WITCH AND ASTRAL EXORCIST

WICKED THREATS

IDENTIFY ENEMIES, PSYCHIC ATTACKS, BLACK MAGICK, CURSES AND DARK FORCES

MELINDA KAY LYONS
"Melinda The Mystic Witch"

ABOUT THE AUTHOR

Melinda Kay Lyons is a host and producer of her YouTube channel, 'Melinda the Mystic Witch.' where she helps millions from malicious metaphysical threats worldwide through her work. Her focus is to enlighten others on divination, ascension, psychic powers, witchcraft, demonology, angelology, the God-particle and more. In 2020 Melinda posted a YouTube video on her channel stating her psychic premonitions of the infamous trial between Johnny Depp and Amber Heard. Her psychic insight gained attention and was featured in a Discovery+ and HBO MAX documentary series, Johnny vs Amber in 2022.

Melinda works with benevolent/ neutral deities only and firmly believes in the law of karma and the power of love guided by truth. She currently lives in the state of Alaska and continues to practice her craft in the comfort of the last frontier. When she's not writing books or producing videos, she's creating and selling her custom mystic products.

To contact Melinda or for more information:
www.LastFrontierMedium.com

Connect with Melinda on Instagram/ @MelindaMysticWitch

WITCH AND ASTRAL EXORCIST

WICKED THREATS

IDENTIFY ENEMIES, PSYCHIC ATTACKS,
BLACK MAGICK, CURSES AND DARK FORCES

MELINDA KAY LYONS
"Melinda The Mystic Witch"

MKL BOOKS

WICKED THREATS:
IDENTIFY ENEMIES, PSYCHIC ATTACKS, BLACK MAGICK, CURSES AND DARK FORCES

Copyright © 2024 by Melinda Kay Lyons

All portions of this work pertaining to content translation, annotations and notes, original artwork, and any and all other original content are subject to copyright. All rights reserved by the Publisher, whether the whole or part of the material is concerned, specifically the rights of translation, reprinting, reuse of illustrations, recitation, broadcasting, reproduction on microfilms or in any other physical way, and transmission or information storage and retrieval, electronic adaptation, computer software, or by similar or dissimilar methodology now known or hereafter developed. Exempted from this legal reservation are brief excerpts in connection with reviews or scholarly analysis. Duplication of this publication or parts thereof is permitted only under the provisions of the Copyright Law of the Publisher's location, in its current version, and permission for use must always be obtained from Melinda Kay Lyons. Violations are liable to prosecution under the respective Copyright Law.

ISBN: 9798878156844 | NEW EDITION 2024

Publisher: MKL Books
Cover Design: Shutterstock.com & Depositphotos.com
Edited by Melinda Kay Lyons

DISCLAIMER:
The content in hand is intended for entertainment, spiritual, educational purposes only. The author/ publisher of this book is not responsible in any manner whatsoever for any adverse effects arising directly or indirectly as a result of the information provided in this book. If not practiced/ used safely with caution and commonsense, demonology can be spiritually, emotionally, mentally, and physically dangerous to one's health. The concepts and practices presented here are to be used if chosen at your own risk. Melinda Kay Lyons is not responsible for the experiences you obtain from working with the methods presented. The content in this book is based on the author's personal experience and conjecture and published to only educate and not meant to encourage physical, mental, emotional, or spiritual harm.

The gift of freedom and peace does not come
without first fighting for it.

CONTENTS

Introduction   9

PART ONE: LIES VS. REALITY

Chapter 1: Law of Attraction Distraction   19

PART TWO: BANEFUL ENCOUNTERS

Chapter 2: Baneful People   33

Chapter 3: Baneful Locations   81

Chapter 4: Baneful Rituals   117

Chapter 5: Baneful Symbols, Devices, and Idols   135

Chapter 6: Baneful Threats   161

PART THREE: PSYCHIC DEFENSES

Chapter 7: Jewels of Protection   185

Chapter 8: High Defense and Purification   213

Chapter 9: Psychic Empowerment   249

INTRODUCTION

"Psychic attacks are very, very rare..."

You may not be a target by a malevolent spirit, but that doesn't mean it's not happening every day to someone else. Let's not beat around the bush. Let's get straight to the point so I don't waste your time or mine. Both good and evil spirits exist. However, enlightened spiritualists are teaching that negative entities, energies, encounters, and experiences, are due to your thoughts, thus creating the negative moments in your life. When I hear an individual utter the phrase, it pains my heart, "Psychic attacks are very, very, very rare." This is not only utterly incorrect but also an insult to those negatively impacted by psychic attacks. Psychic attacks are an abused sense of energetic power explicitly constructed to target a chosen victim to cause harm, pain, suffering, and even a range of curses or bad luck. Psychic attacks not only do happen, but you may have been a victim of a psychic attack and don't even know it.

I don't know when, where, how, or why this lie started, and it's not remotely necessary. What is essential is understanding and respecting the universal balance in energy frequencies within the cosmos and residing within the consciousness of all individual beings.

Within every human being, there is what we call the soul. The soul is the consciousness of that particular person that takes a home into the human body temporarily. Once the human body dies, the soul transitions into specific vibrations that match that person's consciousness. Every level of consciousness holds exceptional levels of thought and emotional vibrations. Those vibrational waves send out a signal to the universe, immediately identifying the soul's specific energetic vibration. Positive, neutral, and negative energy are the primary frequencies a human soul and other spirits exhibit.

Understanding basic knowledge of energy assists in identifying levels of the energetic state of being within you and the energy around you. Without identifying the energy vibrations, you encounter, it can put you in danger and harm others you love. Energy has a way of either helping us or hurting us. No person on this planet is impenetrable of destructive power and intentional psychic infliction from another.

The occult community is exceptionally gifted, yet hateful individuals set in hostile intentions carry negative energy everywhere they go. This wicked energy will not only make you feel gravely uncomfortable to be around that kind of person but can even cause bodily harm to nightmares. With enough personal practice by taking time to sense the energies around you, you'll become skilled in recognizing when the power in someone is harmful or helpful. This also includes energy in objects and the land you may arrive to.

Everything and everyone embody energy frequencies, and because of this, the energy levels through our thoughts and emotions can also change the energy we represent. Energy can constantly change through our thoughts and feelings. In the Law of Attraction, one brings about what one thinks about. Like attracts like. However, just because you have positive thoughts and emotions doesn't mean so do other people around you. And it's here in the introduction that I have to start this out by saying; it's not all about you.

As unfair as this statement is, please give me a chance to explain further. Yes, this book is absolutely about protecting you and your loved ones from harmful energy and entities. And one must be given the right kind of tips and tools to guard oneself against those opposing forces. However, harmful energies aren't just happening for no apparent reason. The negative energy is in existence because someone or something made it come into existence in the first place. Energy by itself has no emotional attachments thus cannot harm a human soul. However, the energy harnessed, used, and abused by a negative emotion from a person or an entity can become a problem. Energy in itself is neither negative nor positive. It's neutral. Neutral energy means the power is neither good nor bad; instead, it is just energy available to be used how we choose.

A knife, for example, is not an evil kitchen utensil. A knife aims to slice, chop, and separate food to feed our family and create a beautiful editable masterpiece. Knives are not conscious objects and are there for us to use with that exact purpose. However, if a person with evil intentions decides to pick up that knife and inflict it on animals or humans, that's when the utensil becomes a dangerous device.

Energy is similar. Power gives humans the ability to have a warm home with electricity. Energy isn't just in our appliances, though. There are immense amounts of energy surging through your body at this very moment. And that same energy is what gives you the ability to do many of the things you do each day. Power in our bodily machines provides us with the ability to wake up in the morning, eat, jog, get to work, and do other daily tasks in our lives. The energy within your body is there purposefully to engage in your life physically and is charged by the type of emotions, thoughts, and those around us.

Within every religion, there is a conflict between good and evil. All spiritual practices in some form or another harness the respect and understanding that there is light and dark energy. Triggering the human conscience in the realm of the decision through choice and consequence. Depending upon one's mortal journey will lead one to a Utopia or to the Underworld to be tortured by demons for all eternity by a God that ever so loved you. The same religions that speak of Angels that save those who ask for their divine guidance, healing, and protection speak of Devils that rein on the parade of leading humanity down a road to self-destruction through temptation and influence.

Thousands of years before Christianity came into being; other civilizations passed down this fundamental spiritual truth. Some, to name a few, were ancient Egyptian, Babylonian, Sumerian, Mayan, Hinduism, Judaism, Buddhism, Islam, and others throughout history that have carried these traditional beliefs to our modern day. Each religion brought and continues to maintain its version of the supernatural conflict between good and evil and our free will to decide in which we choose to reside.

Different levels of energy frequencies carry their version of what they determine is in their party to be true to them. Like yourself, all spirits are called to align with the type of energy frequency that resonates most to them based on their deepest desires and intentions. As there are energies in the land we walk on, the places we visit, live, and the items we touch, so too are certain levels of energy frequencies that your soul vibrates that reach to the purest potential based on your choices, emotions, thoughts, and actions throughout your life. No amount of activity that is done or emotions one expresses are without the imprint of vibrational frequency.

Legends of Angels and Demons have been the focal point of discussion since man learned the spoken word. Evil from the most heinous of beings capable of doing indescribable horror to the human's imagination. Angels with wings that stretch far as the eye can see with the voice of something like a hymn.

Are these beings real? Do they exist?

Not only do Angels and Demons exist, but they are ever watchful of the human race and the souls that depart. Angels and Demons are based on a hierarchy that corresponds to the necessary guidelines of Heaven and Hell. Both Heaven and Hell are the polar vibrations of benevolence and malevolence that pulses to the beat of good or evil deeds.

Demons work under the structure and authority of Devils. Though Satan exists within the course of the universe, neither is he the only threat upon humanity. There are countless versions of good and evil within the billions of galaxies in the massive universe and within those galaxies lie realms. Within these incomprehensible realms are spirits that condone immoral torment imaginable.

As a Psychic Medium, I've worked with numerous types of spirits. In addition, to Angels, Starseeds, Ascended Masters, like Yehoshua (Jesus Christ) and Gandhi to work with some of the most respected and worshipped benevolent Gods like Shiva, the Great Hindu God, and Anubis, the ancient Egyptian God who assists souls to the transition of here to the afterlife.

With that being said, the basis of one's soul vibration is determined based upon one's love vibration or lack thereof. The purest vibration a person can reside in is within the emotion of love. Love holds within it the power to do the most unimaginable and imaginable things like creating, healing, protecting, empowering, and even more! It is love that all religions encourage the soul to aspire in the order of all things. Love is the ultimate moral compass.

As spiritual beings with a human experience, other supernatural forces crave this energy that both the human race and other sentient beings embody. For within the power of love, holds one highest source of unlimited possibilities giving the gift of ultimate creation to do things beyond any other creature on this planet. -Devils and Demons will stop at nothing to have this energy for themselves! The diabolical plan lies within the soulless hole of the otherworldly beast seeking to find the next victim. No man or child is untouchable to the malice these beings can infringe upon the vulnerable. Seeking the human soul to take for itself for greed is all too tantalizing to the crouching darkness that lurks in every crack and corner of a gloomed space. Heed warning for secondary evil does not always commit without the vulnerability of influence from the primary master of evil.

Each source of dogma verbalizes the core concept of surrendering to a higher power, yielding to a God that will give way to avenge you and your family as long as one is willing to submit to the higher authority.

God's energy is neither evil nor good. For all power receives its vibration by the holder through that master's intentions. When a man commits murder, this is because of the man's choices that lacked the power of love. When a mother protects her child, it's thanks to the love of her heart. God's energy is based on the source of the one that harnesses the power to do good or evil, and it's within all beings that have this power to make it what they choose.

Primitive as religions may be, the interpretation is neither true nor false. The answer lies within you. For within the Lost Gospel of Saint Thomas that was discovered in 1945, were the words spoken from Jesus Christ himself stating,

"...I tell you the truth, Simon, when I say that the Heavenly realm is within you. Only when you have established the divine realm within and overcome the demons of doubt and fear will you discern the Key to the establishment of the realm of Eloheim on the physical plane."

"As a person thinks in his heart, so is he, and so is the world in which he dwells. Every person creates his own world, according to that which he fears and that which he loves..."

Jesus proclaimed that the power and realm of Heaven are inside you and all about you. But, unfortunately, it is apparent that religion today significantly lacks the spiritual and energetic understanding of the human consciousness and intricate underlying psychic abilities that all beings possess.

In this book, you will be given the tools to protect yourself by using your power of love and taking back what is rightfully yours. To regain peace, one must first fight for thy soulful birthright. No woman or man in history prevailed in the heart of war without first understanding their unique talents towards personal empowerment. Here you will learn the importance of understanding how to utilize your power and banish evil for good!

PART ONE:
LIES VS REALITY

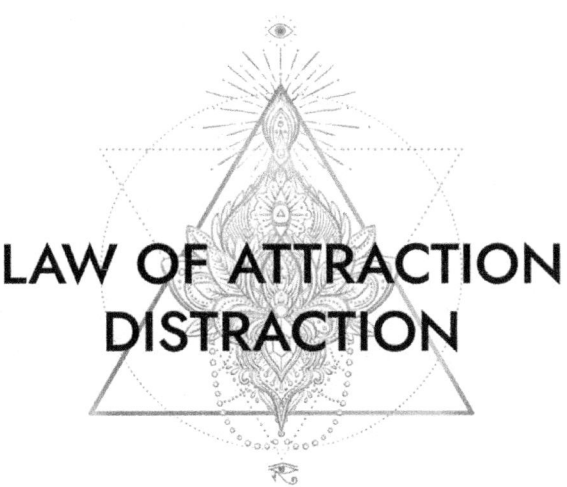

LAW OF ATTRACTION DISTRACTION

CHAPTER ONE

How many spiritual teachers have you seen invest endless hours describing the essence of the Law of Attraction? It seems like it happened overnight, where thousands of spiritual gurus discuss the responsibility of one's thoughts. YouTube alone must have millions of videos on this topic by countless believers, spiritual teachers, and psychics. Perhaps this became a sensation when the film and the famous book The Secret by Rhonda Byrne hit the market. This changed the way people viewed the concept of thought and how powerful thought waves are. Law of Attraction encouraged the viewer to gain emotional responsibility by replacing it with desirable focal outcomes to alter the mind to change one's current circumstances. The Secret was out and spreading like wildfire. The gossip no longer could be contained, and the instructional videos launched into the waves of

YouTube, Facebook, and other social media platforms. There wasn't an author out there that didn't seek to cash in on this mental evolutionary advancement -but is any of it true?

Do our thoughts change our livelihood, and can we have everything we want just by switching our mental state? Can we wake up millionaires just by using the Law of Attraction? If I focus on something hard, long, and passionate enough, will what I concentrate on come into manifestation literally? When bad things happen to me, is it really because I attracted it? Am I really to blame for all of the terrible things that have happened to me? The answer may surprise you.

-Yes. The Law of Attraction is genuine, but few dive deeper into exactly what it is and how it works. As much as we all want to believe that the Law of Attraction could bring us all the money in the world, it's not as effective if not utilized correctly and effectively. The answer is both a yes and a no because there is no possible way to have everything you want simply by thinking about it. The reason for this is simple. -It's not energetically practical nor realistic.

Let's be authentic as possible to gain as much of the genuine feedback you so ever deserve. What you don't earn is being told a bunch of top sale lies that will make you broke buying another, get rich quick scheme. Nor is it fair to say that it is accurate, thus the reason for your attracting too negative experiences into your life.

The Law of Attraction is indeed one of the exceptional subjects that forces your vibration to rise to the occasion on command. We must remember that we are spiritual beings having a physical experience; however, it's not our job to have everything we want physically on demand. If we had everything on demand when we focused on it, it wouldn't allow the human experience to give you what you came here to learn, which are lessons of the human experience.

THE FALSE IDEOLOGY

The Law of Attraction is probably the biggest dilemma in the market within the spiritual community, which makes my job a bit harder. In my work, I discuss the importance of protecting yourself from negative vibrations that may be around when traveling to locations, friend's homes, hotels, or to your workplace. Psychically I'm able to detect a potential threatening energy force in the vicinity that could be harmful. Unfortunately, since the Law of Attraction came into awareness, the public would rather shun the reality of potentially dangerous energy among them.

For example, I had published my first book, Demons and Familiars: A Contemporary Guide of Demonology, with the intention and hope that it would be received well. But, point blank, it wasn't. Whenever I entered a new age store and presented the owner of my book, they turned me away. One store owner refused to much less read my book and even speak to me in person. I got so angry over this that I let her know just how ignorant her thinking was. Every time I attempted to present my book to any store owner, they turned me down without the slightest consideration or conversation. Most often, they sneered at the very presence of myself while walking away, muttering something I'm sure was rude. At first, I assumed it was due to my short stature, being that I'm relatively short for thirty-five, and they more than likely thought I was a rebellious teen. But the more I tried, the more I began to realize it wasn't me at all; it was what they projected on the outside from their judgment. Not only was it disheartening, but I felt like I was defeated. I was defeated in a corner, unable to shine the light on what I was trying to expose, the biggest threat against humanity.

As the eyes of each store owner met the cover that displayed a demon, is when each gave a sign of disgust. The cover of Demons and Familiars: A Contemporary Guide of Demonology is meant to enlighten the reader in the harsh reality that is ever so present. The demon's face on the cover represents the supernatural threats that have existed long before humanity came to earth. Unfortunately, as good as my intentions were, and no matter how polite I was, I was pretty much slammed with a flat-out "No."

The stronghold belief that demons and devils are only attracted to those that talk about them is one of the most outspoken myths ever concocted. Whoever decided to state that as truth -I'd love to give that fool a piece of my mind; it's not only a myth but a lie that has made it all so much easier for evil forces to ever creep into our midst so without us being the wiser. The unrecognizable reality that I will present to you is based upon my own experiences. What you're learning is why the Law of Attraction in terms of spiritual warfare is bullshit.

Excuse me being forward as I wipe away the nonsense that has been smeared upon the millions of minds that will believe anything that's drilled into them. When it looks like BS, smells like BS, and makes you feel like crap -it's most definitely a steaming pile of lies.

Allow the following few pages to enlighten the facts as I assert myself into your attention by saying, not everything you think about is what everyone else is thinking. Within every single person is a place of mental and emotional vibrations. The vibrations within you are not the same as the person standing next to you at the grocery line. That person next to you may not have the same beliefs as you, the same level of awareness of their consciousness, energy, intentional motives, nor on their immediate powers. Not to mention the billions of people all over the world. When you take a moment to consider others in the world, the law of attraction in terms of spiritual warfare seems rather silly. There's no logical way around it. The Law of Attraction in spiritual warfare is not a clear notion, nor does it support the paranormal activity within a faithful and loving home.

VIBRATION ATTRACTION

Every single human being on earth is capable of attracting with their thoughts the experiences that they desire. However, so do those that wish to harm. For example, you may focus on attracting love into your life. You will be picturing the type of personality and physical appearance of this person. Then suddenly, one day, the woman/man of your dreams appears at your door exactly how you envisioned this person to be. As good as this may seem, this doesn't always have a happy beginning or an ending. For the dreamy person at your doorstep very well could turn into your worst nightmare. Nearly half the time, the person you wished to meet may turn out to be someone you weren't expecting and will be the worst surprise of your life. That person very well could've been wanting someone just like you to take advantage of on every level possible. And most often, these types of people do!

There is a sense of like attracts like. Yes, this is true. Absolutely! Two people vibrating on the same frequency level can magically pull towards one another and entwined in love. When the universe works harmoniously through the Law of Attraction, it is not forced but ran in a smooth course and often an unexpected one. When we perceive our ideal partner, pet, job, or experiences, we can bring into our life beautiful surprises that will be hard to believe. It may seem all too good to be true. The power of the universe will most often leave you speechless at how splendid the universe harmonizes into your vibrational match. When the Law of Attraction is at work successfully, you're pulled unexpectedly towards the person you were dreaming of meeting. Most often, this is because both you and the other person were dreaming of the same personalities that you both possess and are. This is a beautiful move within the cosmos and can be celebrated for years to come.

But this isn't always the case in every scene of our lives. The Law of Attraction works towards what we most often dream of having from the deepest parts of the heart and soul. The universe doesn't listen to words; instead, it responds to our minds from the mental pictures of the thoughts produced. When the mental images are projected, the universe picks up on the emotional database and understands how it makes us feel. Emotions supported with mental images will make the Law of Attraction work faster and most effectively with the help of our desire fueled by passion.

The Law of Attraction is not only valid; it is a way we can have things suddenly work in our favor at the most reasonable times when we need it most. When you look back at your life, I'm sure you'd find at least once the Law of Attraction working in your favor.

What doesn't work in your favor are spiritual teachers instilling immense guilt over your conscience from terrible happenings that you have no control over.

LAW OF FREE WILL

Those store owners lack the fundamentals of the universal Law of Free Will. Within this law embodies the undoubted responsibility of each human to take the reins of their life one hundred percent. Every human is a spiritual being having a human experience, thus being empowered to make sound choices that will affect them positively, negatively, or neutral. Without respect to this law, would be the enslavement of life -which is exactly what the opposing force would instead enforce.

There are over 100 billion galaxies in the observable universe that correspond not just to the Law of Attraction but in respect of the Law of Free Will. The Law of Free Will states...

"No being has the right to take away the rights of another's decisions or actions. It's in the credibility of one's vibration to make what they will in their free will. Therefore, every being has the freedom of choice based on divine individualism and vibration."

-The Law of Free Will directs attention to spiritual truth for humanity and other beings in the universe. We are not without watchful eyes that linger in the light or the dark. Entities of the highest vibration correcting the wrongs of those in the lowest of realms, while malevolent forces break this universal law. As the Law of Free Will allows these mysterious invisible beings to make their mark without a sound, the understanding of this rule is without question. Lest not be tempted in the grave of naivety, for those responsible for enforcing these laws is ever watchful. They are protecting humans from dusk till dawn. While we awake or lay our heads to rest, the greatest of Angels, Starseeds, and other benevolent forces seek to not only command but enforce this law without hesitation.

SPIRITUAL WARFARE

Spiritual warfare goes farther than what Christianity has portrayed. Ancient Egyptians practiced witchcraft that was concerned with protecting themselves from violent spirits and demons that reveled in the killing of the living and found delight in the torture of the dead. Demons and Devils are found in some of the most ancient civilizations and spiritual practices. We may assume that Christianity adopted most of what is considered folly, but the evidence speaks for itself as one dives into the darkened tunnel of the old ways. The demon belief within ancient Mayans, Samarians, Babylonians not only surpass the age of Christianity but prove its infancy shaped humanity's awareness of these dangerous entities.

Spiritual warfare is not just a "Christian thing" -it's an everyone thing. Spiritual warfare coincides with the two previous laws: the Law of Attraction and the Law of Free Will. Within the Law of Attraction, we can attract negative or positive forces based on our vibrations. However, the Law of Free Will allows one to invite excellent or evil into our lives. Not all who read this may entirely understand unless one has been through spiritual warfare before. One cannot simply comprehend nor thoroughly respect the magnitude of the powerful entities of other dimensions have unless they came face to face with the unnatural threat. All that lives and breathes on earth has a vibration of its own due to the soul attached within the body's temporary hold. Within the body is a soul that holds immense power to create something supreme or destroy to the most extreme. Within the universe, other-dimensional beings that observe humans know this all too well - and also know that most humans are not aware of just how much power they possess!

The Law of Attraction demonstrates the power of one vibration being pulled to another in the exact likeness. However, the positive vibration of one human being doesn't permit only positive entities to encounter the human. It also doesn't enable only good energies to impact the human. Due to the Law of Free Will, no matter the vibration of the human or their thoughts and intentions, the demon and other hostile forces are allowed to invest into the human's life. The demon is not breaking any spiritual laws. The demon is granted the same privilege of Free Will within these universal laws. Thus, it doesn't prevent it from crossing the barrier of benevolence to commit the most heinous acts mercilessly.

Opposing this understanding, most are under the misconception that the human must first invite the demon or devil for the evil to become attached or attracted -this is also a myth and a reckless one.

The demonstration of a demon is vital for one to identify what is at stake. Negative energy exists and can become conscious through the host like a demon or a devil spirit. Though power is not harmful nor positive by itself, the consciousness of a spiritual being can trans mutate that energy into their mindful likeness. As one harnesses hate and jealousy, that energy becomes the adaptation of the thoughts produced from the human or being. Angels make their energy positive through loving thoughts and kind actions. Angels surpass the highest levels of frequency within the vibration of love. Demons, on the contrary, cooperate from the determination of hatred, malice, and evil deeds, thus creating doom within them. Demons and Angels not only do exist but are also functioning their energetic faculties throughout every single action, thought, and emotion. Demons will never become more than what they are, for their very existence lies below the surface of morality.

Spiritual warfare is upon you, whether you accept it or not. And no one is immune to the chaos of the other-dimensional beings that walk our planet in close observation. Conscious monsters are bred for a single purpose integrated with the diabolical dedication to seeking the destruction of the human race.

POSITIVE ATTRACTS NEGATIVE

I hear this all too often, "As long as I have positive thoughts and vibration, I will never attract negative or evil forces." As attractive as this may be, this is not only false but irresponsible. Yes, we can attract positive people and experiences into our lives with positive energy, but that doesn't protect you from the evil that takes advantage of your energy. One cannot simply walk into the world without acknowledging the threats that are among them.

If one encounters a person with a gun pointing at them, instincts would tell that one is in danger of harm or worse. This instinct is due to the Divine Message Receiver that is also called intuition. Intuition is what tells us within our energy whether we are in danger or not. Without this, we would not be able to take heed in protecting ourselves from harm. Likewise, animals and insects of all shapes and sizes carry this intelligent agency of vigorous defense that aids their protection from a predator or other immediate danger. So, whenever a person says this to me, I cannot help but chuckle at the lack of personal accountability that has been within our soul DNA before we incarnated.

I've encountered and have endured some of the worst types of people and beings and suffered from long years of depression from the happenings in my life. Though this is coming from experience, it put me into a place where I blamed myself. Whenever I heard a person recite the Law of Attraction, it frankly angered me so much to the point this book had to be written finally.

After years of deep meditation and spiritual encounters with my Spirit Guides in the other realms, I've learned that no matter who you are or where you come from, you are not responsible for the bad things that have happened to you. Bad people do bad things because they seek to take advantage of easily manipulated or abused. And though hurt people hurt people, it doesn't still blame the victim of the crime. When those in positive vibrations are high in frequency, the lower vibrations of people and spirits will become attracted to them. And in a sense, rightfully so! Negative energy lacks much potency in love, forgiveness, mercy, joy, and other positive emotions. So negative vibrations, both humans and otherworldly beings, will become attracted to the opposite.

It's not in nature for positive forces to become attracted to negative energy. Positivity vibrates with the notion of a moral compass thus walks on the path of pure righteousness. Negativity lacks morality; therefore, it wants to use the positive by abusing it every chance it gets.

Protection of the right type against opposing forces is where you will have a greater sense of advantage. With the right tips and awareness, you will be able to not only recognize threats a mile away but know how to stop it before it goes beyond the barrier of safety. Keep your friends close and your enemies closer. Of course, I can't say that you will never be in harm's way. But the more you learn about the potential unnatural and human threats; you will gain a stronger intuition and confidence than you ever thought possible.

PART TWO:
BANEFUL ENCOUNTERS

BANEFUL PEOPLE

CHAPTER TWO

Everything on earth emits a specific vibration. All that is grown from the globe gives off a precise vibrational pulse allowing an exact aurific tone that corresponds within the trees, flowers, weeds, rocks, and even the water that rushes down into the depths of the dark blue. We are vibrational energy, connected by energy pulses that create our soul makeup. Energy cannot be destroyed but only transitions and trans mutates into another energetic code form. Humans and other sentient beings receive and give off an energy signal that allows the universe to correspond accordingly to the variations of energy currents we embody. So do objects with no sense of liveliness to create an energetic signal. Everything that is both physical and metaphysical shares energy within the cosmos. Everything has its energy flow.

With that in mind, it would be wise to consider the people, places, objects, and even entities one may encounter. Not every person emits positive energy. As much as one would like to believe this, unfortunately, this is not the case. In reality, a person's positive or negative point is based on the host's internal dialog, passion, and lifestyle. Due to the fact energy is within every living being and thing, it's fair to suggest one must take extreme precaution when in the presence of hostile energetic forces that wish you harm. Harmful energy doesn't always happen by accident; in fact, evil energy forces are often from the host that manifested the destructive metaphysical tide with malicious intentions instilled within it.

There's an unspoken truth that no matter how nice someone may appear on the outside doesn't mean they don't desire to set your world upside down. Unfortunately, most folks don't want to admit it when someone just gives them bad vibes -especially in the spiritual community. Many individuals would rather see the good in everyone when in reality, they aren't permitting the truth to be exposed. Not all people are well intended, nor should they ever be trusted. Naïve minds are unaware of just how mischievously certain diabolical characters can be when you piss them off just enough or somehow get on their nerves. There are negatively charged people in the world that will stop at nothing to allow hatred to control their very will to see your life crumble at their feet. Hatred takes over the mind in such a way that it consumes their very soulful vibration, leading them down a path of no return if taken too far. These are the types of people who seek nothing but revenge; hostile ends met with a sick pleasure in seeing your worst fears come to life.

This section will explore the most common negatively charged encounters, movements, and occult practices. People who align themselves to these lifestyles or beliefs are not all evil intended people. Not all who align themselves within these are labeled as the same. Not all people think alike, regardless of their chosen paths. This list does not suggest a negative stereotype or a prejudiced mentality.

However, some are aligned by certain occult practices and movements that should not be taken lightly. There are many types of people that are not a force to underestimate.

TOXIC PEOPLE

When a hurricane is estimated to be headed toward a specific area, there are bound to be a few noteworthy signs—increasing winds, temperature changes, rain, lightning, with your occasional hail and monstrously high tides. Unfortunately, though a storm is easily identifiable, it's not always easy to predict where it is headed. Thankfully with the right hurricane experts, the public is given a warning in advance to get to safety before the storm hits. But, unfortunately, you could be sitting next to a hurricane in your very home and not even realize it.

As there are toxic influences and situations, there are toxic people. This can range from your local store owner, a coworker, your neighbor to family members in the home. For all you know, you very well could be the toxic one in your family and may not know if you are.

The length of egoic energy measures toxicity. A negative and entitled mindful attitude belittles others and raises the bar of your flex. Toxic people cause hateful and even dangerous situations, like criminal activity. This can range from gang activity, physical abuse, sexual abuse to mental or emotional abuse. Those who participate in illegal activity like stealing, drug relations, or riots will embody a highly negative motivation to take away from others they feel entitled or superior to.

Toxicity isn't measured purely upon the person's academics but what is happening to the body. A person that suffers from an eating disorder, depression, addiction, and even some mental disorders can quickly impact an individual's aurific field, causing it to become hostile to themselves or others. After a person has been suffering from a specific grievance for so long, their mind can emit energy that attacks another person's aura, leaving them without a way to defend themselves. Power has a way of knowing what we lack or need. The energy within our aurific field will do its best to suffice what it's lacking. Still, in a prolonged state of negative energy, it can churn that energy into a form of dark, murky energy that's unable to heal itself on its own.

A person dealing with drug addiction, for example, is not only suffering from the addiction itself but from the mindful helplessness that leaves them lingering in depression, hopelessness, helplessness, and lack of self-love. When this occurs, the suffering addict begins to abuse more drugs due to the addiction consuming their very will to resist and live a healthy life. Nothing matters to the addict anymore, only the high. The high is all that matters and is the only thing that will keep the addict going. Sadly, the addict is unaware that the addiction kills them physically and soulfully. The energy of an addict becomes so descended in sorrow and helplessness due to the addict's emotional database that's being triggered by the drug repeatedly. These emotions are what bury the addict over and over in an endless cycle of no return. The addict must cut the negative attachment to the drug willingly through their free will, with the help of those that will give them support. This is what must be done for the addict to become a survivor. Painful. This battle is not easily won and must be fought repeatedly for the suffering addict to remain clean of the negative attachment.

Granted, I'm not a doctor and have no say in anything about addiction, but energetically, addiction to drugs, alcohol, objects, and even sex will consume the person on a metaphysical scale that is sometimes beyond repair.

Not all of those things may be of concern; sometimes, it's simply the person's lifestyle and personality. Unfortunately, people in this world want nothing good for others because they live miserable lives. Misery loves company thus will sit alongside grief and allow it to consume them. These personalities focus on life and experiences as the glass is half empty instead of half full. They're never satisfied with anything they receive while releasing endless lines of dissatisfactory results. Their levels of shallow expectations will reap the benefits of no man or woman, for there is no way to make them happy or satisfied. These people will never become happy or seek a way to make happiness a part of their lives. They find blame in every scenario in the face of others but never take ownership of their own choices. In these types of personalities, we psychics call **Psychic Vampires** that we will cover later.

The characteristic of an individual's mindfulness can either create positive energy or negative energy depending on the type of thoughts one makes in mind. As we covered before, the host creates positive and negative energy -the person. For example, simply hating on another for biased or prejudiced reasons will manifest hateful dark power within them. Wicked thoughts and emotions lead to cruel and destructive actions, and hurtful actions leave everyone suffering from low vibrational energy.

Toxic people come in all different forms. There is no one-size-fits-all when it comes to identifying a poisonous individual. The negative feelings you will experience when around the person who emits the toxic fume remain.

TOXIC GROUPS | MOVEMENTS | CULTS

Negatively charged groups like Black Lives Matter are prime examples of today's generation of evil movements. Although on the outside, the phrase may appear strong and bold for those of color, the narrative prohibits social justice freedom of speech and permits violence to be the voice of the "movement." In addition, social justice warriors or the "woke" mentality within politics can also harbor a placement of social inequality, thus striking venomous arrows to hit the heart of the young, the vulnerable, and the influential.

Every ethnicity deserves equality, justice, and even some form of reparations to repair the injustices that happened in history. Racism is a reality everyone faces on all scales that should be taken seriously on every level respectably. As good as intended as the movement of Black Lives Matter appears to be -that is not the motivational purpose of this group. I'm not going to go deep into political views or the dark agenda of it all, but what must be pointed out are the horns on the multibillion-dollar lie that has ruined millions of lives. Not only did Black Lives Matter instill into the minds of adults the idea that rioting was acceptable, but too has it been engraved in the minds of our teens and children. These types of mentalities create division. Division against humanity cannot do anything positive when its entire agenda is against humans of all ethnicities.

On May 25, 2020, a Black man named George Floyd died by a police officer's knee on his neck. It was a sad day for America and all over the globe. The tragic event happened to be recorded and subjected to everyone worldwide. Everyone all over the nation was talking about it and still is today. This was a murder recorded on the grounds of American soil by the very people who swore to protect and preserve the rights of civilians in the community. George Floyd's death was not only unfair but inhumane. George Floyd's life was taken away by people who took an oath to protect and serve the community and nation. However, not all people are perfect, and what these men did will suffer from their decisions for the rest of their lives. At the same time, George will never be with his family and friends, grieving his loss for years to come.

In the heat of reaction and escalated anger, people began to protest in the name of George Floyd. In a violent strike against Black and Brown people being killed by the hands of police officers. They were demanding to defund the police or reform if their fists did not set abolishment in the air. When protests weren't enough, riots ravaged the towns, cities, and homes. Riots destroyed communities without warning. Thousands of people became victims from the BLM shirt wearer yelling racial profanities at the innocent elderly Caucasian couple. The protestor quickly became the rioter when yelling and screaming weren't enough. Raiding and pillaging everything in their path to set the record straight that they were done being victims of police abuse. I will never forget the endless videos on social media. One could not escape the violent rampage against anyone that wasn't in the "movement."

The Black Lives Matter movement is toxic and promotes terrorism beyond repair. These "protestors" did riot entire towns, homes, and people's lives. I witnessed some of the victims who shared how they lost family members caught in the crossfire of the mindless destruction.

Black lives do matter without question. But a movement that exhibits and supports only one type of race causes diversity. One should be reminded of the notorious Adolf Hitler, who proclaimed his social justice movement to reparations. The same link connects the same toxic mentality that infested millions of minds to kill millions of innocent men, women, and children. When a movement focuses solely on race, one will soon be racing to erase a race. The moment BLM members raised their fists into the air, all I heard was the word "Hitler." As much as one wouldn't want history to repeat itself, the truth remains that when you begin to erase history, you are destined to repeat it. And that's just what BLM has attempted to do: change history entirely instead of focusing on the facts.

Other groups aligned in defamation of the human race are the Ku Klux Klan, The Black Panthers, ANTIFA, Neo-Nazis, and other hate groups. Religions like Scientology, Mormonism, Jehovah's Witnesses, and many others that permit sexual abuse, physical abuse, isolation of their family members, members of the groups, and total control over their lives are noteworthy additions of toxic cults. Just because religion was created to serve a higher power doesn't mean its focus isn't on the lower ends.

Critical Race Theory is a theory and cult-like ideology that, in 2021, has become the beacon of what appears to be a new threat against Caucasians and anyone that disagrees with the dark motives. Critical Race Theory isn't a religious group yet still holds to the toxicity in alleging to terminate and even kill those who reject the racist agenda. CRT in itself harmonized with something like the KKK in the modern-day and must be avoided at all costs. Troubling, Critical Race Theory is instilling into the minds of children in schools that basically no matter what, a white person is a racist and was born a racist due to the inherent racism that was given to them through their bloodline. CRT slowly emerged to the public in 2020 (CRT was years earlier) during the coronavirus pandemic, which has led people to panic at the thought that this theory could bring them to this hopeless demise. -This is another cult-like mentality that is being pressured and pushed into the minds of our younger generation that will ultimately cause segregation of families with the disapproval of racial opinions.

These groups, cults, ideologies, and others not mentioned, or ones that may birth in the future of similar nature, are not groups or movements of a higher purpose. Instead, these groups strive to divide and conquer nations and countries, and its people to take control of those they feel are superior. Not only are these groups extremely toxic, but they are filled and fueled by people that fully believe and live by the repulsive immorality and inhumane mentalities.

PSYCHIC VAMPIRES

Have you ever met a person that seemed to just suck the life out of you? Though you spent only a few minutes, maybe an hour with this person, even with a somewhat good experience, you still found yourself departing with a sense of energy depletion? If you've experienced this, you've encountered a real living psychic vampire. Excuse the Dracula bit because this isn't it.

Psychic vampires are living people that drain your energy frequency to the point of utter exhaustion. The energy drainage is that you cannot help but feel like no matter how much sleep you get or how much coffee you drink, you're still tired beyond measure. Psychic vampires are individual human beings that will steal the energy that surrounds them and more—stealing power from people, animals, happy situations, emotions, memories, and locations. Unfortunately, the psychic vampires aren't aware that they're the energy thief that's been taking the fun out of everything and everyone, everywhere they go. Instead, they will usually blame everyone else while delivering the negativity to your very doorstep or workplace.

It's palpable the more you're with a psychic vampire, for the evidence cannot help but reveal itself the longer you're around or live with this person. It's not uncommon for families to have at least one psychic vampire. Not just the immediate family, but the entire family line will have at least one or two psychic vampires within the family tree. Psychic vampires are most known to carry specific negative personality traits. These personalities consist of narcissists, abusive behaviors, master manipulators, psychopaths, sociopaths, severe apathetic tendencies, a manic-bipolar disorder that isn't treated medically, schizophrenia, and many other areas not mentioned.

(Not everyone with mental disorders is a psychic vampire, but without proper treatment and psychological help from a certified professional, this is often the case.)

Individuals that also suffer from addiction tend to be psychic vampires due to their lacking accountability or ability to withstand the habit. Addiction takes away the human's capabilities to retain any sense of being human in itself. It controls all of the person's sense of decision-making, empathy, and judgment in those decisions. Though they may have love within their big heart, the psychic vampire tends to become the victim of their misfortunes. The very notion of the world versus them often leaves anyone in their presence to drown in the misery from the "poor me" mentality.

To be fair, most individuals who are psychic vampires don't mean to be, for they lack awareness of how their mental state and behaviors affect those around them. And attempting to inform the person of their vampiric ways, you may be left with a door slammed in your face. Not always will a psychic vampire listen to your words of care or concern, especially in the areas of psychic attacks. Without awareness, they subject others and even pets to losing their life force without being the wiser.

The psychic vampire must be avoided at all costs, or at least as often as you can spare. Though it may be your mother, father, brother, sister, son, daughter, or even your loving spouse, the damage can be too significant to escape if not caught in time. Energy taken too often from a person causes a range of psychical discomforts and mental and physical instability not just to the psychic vampire but to anyone that's around them. Being around a psychic vampire too long can infiltrate exceptional damage to your mind, body, and soul energy. It will start small, like headaches, dizziness, and fainting spells. Over time, however, your emotional and mental state will worsen as you develop depression, anxiety, paranoia, nightmares, all the way to going deaf, blindness to severe illnesses like tumors, cancer, sudden death, or suicide.

(Having a physical disability does not automatically label you a psychic vampire victim. It's based on one's energy vibrations.)

Simply being on the phone with a psychic vampire, exchanging texts and emails can and will affect you psychically and physically. The more you converse with a psychic vampire, you'll notice that your mannerisms begin to change and are unlike who you initially are. **Empaths** are prone to be significantly affected by the vampire due to the psychic ability of the empathic person picking up on every ounce of the vampire's toxicity. The Empath is a gifted individual with an extrasensory psychic ability to feel everything others are going through. This is one of the most influential and beautiful parts of psychic abilities, for it allows the Empath to empathize with what others around them are suffering from entirely. However, the more an Empath is around psychic vampires, the greater the chances the Empath will lose themself. They will lose their sense of identity, leaving their authentic self behind. Empathic people can sense emotions, physical illnesses, injuries, thoughts, and even other people's history through this psychic ability. It's been spoken that Empaths are not psychic -this is false! Empathic skills are of great importance for the psychic to sense the emotional stability of others and the history in locations through the dead.

    Psychic vampires are among us but not through only the living. Spirits like departed human souls that have died, too, can become psychic vampires. This is common when a location is haunted, or a specific human soul has cursed land before their earth departure. Ill-minded human souls, or Ghosts, can develop a negative mindset when exposed to too much negativity. This negativity can range from other spirits around or the living they haunt. If the residence is involved in criminal activity, abuse, or different toxicity levels, the dead human spirit will begin to suck the energy of those they haunt. The living most often isn't aware of what is happening and will blame other sensible reasons to find the cause—leaving the living human unable to shake off the negative attached spirit without the energy of their own or the ability to fight it off properly. Other spirits that are not human can and are often psychic vampires to the most extreme. Other entities include Poltergeist Manifestations, Witch Creatures (entities created through magick), Gremlins, Trolls, Witchdoctors, Shadow People, UFO, Reptilians, Demons, Devils, and other descended entities.

Psychic vampires lack positive energy, so they take all the power they encounter. Though one can shield from the vampire's fangs, the shield lasts for only so long. The psychic vampire's forceful pull can and will rupture your psychic defense leaving one vulnerable to further harm. Unless one is willing to continually safeguard themselves daily, which can be mentally tiring itself, it's advisable for long-term health safety concerns that the psychic vampire is left in their cave alone as often as possible or banished for good.

Of course, it's not my place or anyone's place to tell you who you should have in your life, especially when it comes to one's loved ones. No one should be given that kind of power or flexibility. Therefore, it's my opinion and advisory that it would be best to avoid those you feel may be a psychic vampire as much as needed for your spiritual well-being. Further in the book, we will discuss protecting yourself from psychic vampires if you choose to keep the individual in your life.

THE SATANIST

There are two kinds of Satanists, the Atheistic Satanist, and the Theistic Satanist. Philosophical Satanists believe in the heavily indoctrinated aesthetic component, a system through symbolism metaphor through rituals in which Satan is embraced not as a Devil God to be worshipped but as a symbol of external projection of the highest potential of each Satanist. A Satanist in accurate alignment will state Satanism is based on love and kindness. A kindness not wasted upon those that don't deserve it and vengeance for those that earned it.

Anton Szandor LaVey, the founder and high priest of the Church of Satan, rallied allies to assert that Satanism is not for the weak-minded, only for those willing to take full responsibility for their lives. He was tearing down the notion of Psychic Vampires as nonsense and the belief in demons or devils literally. Though Anton subjected his followers to what is now considered philosophical Satanism, his work remains controversial. "Hail Satan" would be spoken during alleged rituals, instigated with naked men and women in orgies and blood ceremonies held practically daily before his death, on October 29th, 1997. People worldwide would believe in his dark rituals as philosophical when this is not the case in psychical understanding.

Theistic Satanists view Satan as a supernatural deity, seeing him not as omnipotent but rather as a patriarch. In contrast, Atheistic Satanists regard Satan as merely a symbol of certain humanistic traits and behaviors. Theistic Satanists take Satan and demons literally without apologies as their rituals commence. Theistic Satanism roughly consists of depraved satanic rituals guided in extreme perversion. Occasional orgies through sex magick, demon worship, demonic summoning, invocation, and the evocation to the levels of sacrifice. Sacrifice doesn't always include a life of a sentient being -but that's how evil always starts. A sacrifice of one's likeness like food or a particular simple pleasure to satisfy the demon during your suffering is considered to most Theistic Satanists as an acceptable sacrifice. Sacrificial rituals are not always a required means of summoning nor through the summoning of a demon or a devil. Instead, the desperation makes a sacrifice of the human host that plays the role of the dutiful Satanist willing to sacrifice their very morals to gain what they ask of the descended entity.

Many Satanists will state they don't condone sacrificial rituals but will operate within the lines of **Bloodletting** if tolerable. Bloodletting is the shedding, drinking, desecration of human or animal blood, or even cannibalism. Though not all Satanists align themselves to this primitive insanity of rituals, many still practice it today. The isolation of a Satanist long enough with only the contact and communication with other depraved minds like demons and devils leads one to further inhumane behaviors and agendas.

Respectfully, many Satanists have extraordinary minds, hearts, and souls. The issue, however, is it doesn't matter what the Satanist believes what Satanism is, for their own opinion doesn't equate to the minds of devils or demons. So again, it's not the mind of the Satanist that matters in this situation; it's the influence of the demon that matters when it comes to the Satanist. A Satanist doesn't become a Satanist overnight. Though many feel they've made this "religious" choice on their own, this is not the case for **Demonic Influence**, which is also based on the four Demonic Stages that I discuss in my book, *Demons, and Familiars: A Contemporary Guide of Demonology*. Demons and Devils counteract all the human does. Everything the human believes or does, the demon and devil will fill the mind of the human target to dominate their own beliefs. This is done slowly. Though most horror and paranormal films will make this process appear fast, it's prolonged so that none will be the wiser -especially the future vowed Satanist.

There was an instance where I encountered one particular Satanist who considered himself an Atheistic Satanist. In an engaging enlightening conversation with him, we began exchanging the difference in opinion in a respectful manner. From talking with him and hearing from his point of view, I learned he didn't believe demons or devils were necessarily evil spirits. It was confusing to me, but I respected his opposition and him, nonetheless.

He was unlike most Satanists I've met, honestly. He was kind, generous, very polite, and never seemed arrogant whenever I mentioned something of my understanding of the spirit world. Frankly, his energy isn't typically how a Satanist approaches me. He was different than the others. So different that it told me he didn't belong in Satanism.

That very night when I got home and went to sleep, I suddenly found myself being pulled onto the astral realm and psychically attacked by what appeared to look like a demonic witchdoctor. I've never encountered this spirit before nor sense, and what I remember vividly is having to call on Archangel Michael to rescue me. This unpleasant guest grabbed me and began to throw me around my room violently without warning! His eyes were bursting red, supercharged in energy velocity that I'd not witnessed before. It was magick that electrified within his aura so aggressively that it sounded like power surged within his voice as he spoke. His very presence was aggressive and full of malice. What felt like a few seconds too long, once I called upon Archangel Michael, his benevolent force dashed into the space of my astral room in golden white light to my defense. Archangel Michael and other light beings banished the demonic witchdoctor for good. The instant the entity was banished, my guides placed me back to my physical form, where I awoke with bruises on my body. So struck with alarm that it took hours to shut my eyes once more.

    The very next morning, I sent a message to the same Satanist and told him what had happened to me—explaining what the demon witchdoctor did and what it said. Going into detail how the demon furiously said as it was attacking me that I should stay away from the Satanist (him). When I gave details of this demon, the Satanist confirmed that this was the entity that he was working with. The Satanist never told me anything personal about the types of spirits he worked with before my attack. I never bothered to ask either because it's none of my business, and frankly, I didn't think this would happen. After discussing my recent attack and the appearance of this demonic witchdoctor, the Satanist confirmed this was the same spirit he confided in. Not only was the Satanist left speechless, but so was I. Neither of us had encountered such a reckless situation in this scenario before. Once we agreed it was the same spirit, I tried to convince him to stay away from this demon and why it wasn't in his best interest. Unfortunately, no matter what I said, he refused to take my advice and even proclaimed that maybe the demon wasn't his but from somewhere else. He retracted everything he stated and made me look paranoid, even though he affirmed it was the same demon a few moments ago.

    After about an hour's talk on Facebook, I immediately decided not to see or talk to him anymore. He wasn't interested in cutting this demon from his life and was uninterested in anything I had to say about it. He didn't understand why I refused to see him anymore, though I clearly defined that when a person's demon attacks me -it's over. No questions asked, no second thoughts.

DONE. When you work with demons, and you clearly don't show any empathy for the attack, it's evident that the devil has a hold on the person and isn't thinking for themselves anymore.

Those that walk in the Left-Hand path are set in a current that isn't morally right. For example, a relationship with a Satanist, either Theistic or Atheistic, never usually goes well due to their demons. Even if the Satanist doesn't believe in demons or devils -it doesn't matter. Demons and devils exist, and they believe in our inability to know what is happening before our very presence entirely.

The biggest issue I have in an argument with a Satanist, which often happens on my YouTube channel or in other encounters, is the person struggles to understand that their beliefs do not make up the energetic makeup of a demon. Just because the Satanist doesn't believe in rape or murder doesn't mean the devil won't rape them or their family. Demons and devils possess their ideology outside our realm of morals and empathy. These beings don't take 'no' for an answer when challenged by the Satanist's moral code. They will stop at nothing to ensure that Satanists will eventually accept the diabolical behavior. Atheistic Satanists on a global scale undermine the reality of demonic power. And because they don't believe in demons, to begin with, they use the philosophies as a representation of the demonic entity to highlight their morals -when in common sense, this doesn't make any sense logically. One doesn't need to become a Satanist to have a moral code. The irony that one would become a Satanist when demons themselves don't have morals is the topping to Satan's cake.

As we go further into this book, we dive deeper into the realm of demonology. As a Demonologist, it's my job to identify when a demon is in the vicinity in a person's home, workplace, or, in this case, their religion. When one encounters a Satanist, you'll begin to notice things about their character that may seem darker and less pleasant than the norm. Not in any way to make a negative stereotype on their person or heart. Many Satanists have the biggest hearts out there and will do everything for their family, friends, and even strangers, which is the exact reason why I continue to fight tooth and nail in explaining why they don't belong in Satanism.

Satanism is for those that cannot express empathy whatsoever. Satanism, to the core, is the exact demonic expression and retaliation against anything good, loving, positive, and just. Satanism in plain language is the devil's religion and continues to reign in deceiving millions of people every day. The more an individual exposes themselves with complete vulnerability to Satanism, the energy exchange they will receive from the devils and demons begins to intertwine with theirs. Satanists sadly don't know this when it happens because their third eye is often closed or blocked from the demon. After all, the devil wants to take complete control of the person's psychic abilities. The more the demon has complete control of this person psychically, the more they're capable of taking full control of the person mentally, physically, and emotionally. This can lead to depression, anger tendencies, hostility, mindless hatred, aggressiveness, manic episodes, bipolar disorder, sleep paralysis, massive energy drainage, suicidal thoughts, and thoughts of hurting others.

Some Satanists say Satanism has significantly and positively changed their life for the better. They are sharing their experiences with getting better jobs, no longer involved in toxic relationships, to finding themselves in a more profound spiritual bond within themselves or the entities. It all sounds superb on the outside, but internally, underneath it is a hierarchy of demons working ever so closely on **Infesting, Oppressing,** and **Influencing** this person to get them exactly where they want them before the end goal **Possession.**

Clever the Satanist may be, it takes wisdom to see past the lies and the manipulation of Satanism at its core. Satanism undermines human decision-making, causing the person to be unable to do anything without the guidance of their demon, devil, or religion. Satanism is ultimately a dark cult that consists of individuals choosing to walk in the Left-Hand path. Those that speak of the Left-Hand course explain it as an act of righteousness against Christianity—spitting on the church's doorstep leaving behind the indoctrinated cage of mindless, brainless sheep trailing behind the butcher to their fate. Though I speak of Angels and Demons and speak highly of the dark realities of Demonology, I surprisingly agree with the many Satanist's reasons for leaving Christianity. However, the decision to suddenly join its opposing force is gravely concerning. The issue isn't whether or not they disagree with Christianity; the problem is that the Satanists chose Satanism regardless of their difference in Christianity. Out of all of the religions one could join, why would Satanism be the only choice for the Satanist? Here is the prime example of where the demon led the person to Satanism all along.

Those exploring satanism eventually regret it or meet with doom. Take the endless satanic cult leaders and satanic serial killers, for example. During what is widely known as the **Satanic Panic through** the 1970s-1980s, America and other parts of the world were raving over the sudden fear and paranoia of satanism becoming a prevalent sinister organization among large groups and singular individuals. American pop culture was deeply integrated into the occult, and many Americans believed that the occult was infiltrating the minds of the youth into adults. Parents dreadful of the idea of their children playing games that had anything to do with magick, witchcraft, the music industry, and the lyrics that had to do with the devil to something as simple a child's television show, like the Smurfs was suddenly demonic. Thoroughly the community stepped in, and parents and folks within the police department began to take notice of the potential warning signs of this type of sinister agenda. Of course, most Satanists and your occasional atheist will suggest the Satanic Panic was nothing more than a ridiculous hysteria from paranoid religious parents and those within the church -*but were they wrong to worry?*

As the months turned into years, the satanic killings of victims were soon turning into a game-changer for evil's capability. People were starting to see the truth of how satanism was leading the perpetrator astray from a humanistic moral compass. Police reports from witnesses and further satanic findings from the crime scenes were sending alarm bells not only to the everyday citizen but to those responsible for identifying the culprit in the killings. Satanism was becoming the motivation for more satanic cults, and killers like Ricky Kasso during the Satanic Panic. Ricky Kasso, "The Acid King," was charged with an alleged satanic ritualistic killing and committed suicide in his jail cell. It all started when Kasso began experimenting with drugs like marijuana and hashish, but quickly he escalated to the addiction to LSD and PCP. It didn't take Kasso long before diving into the occult and satanism. He began digging into old graveyards, allegedly searching for an Indian skeleton he intended to steal. When I researched this, it immediately reminded me of **Necromancy**, the darkest form of Satanic workings on Dark Magick an individual could ever go. Necromancy is essentially the workings of magick with a human or animal corpse to do Black magick with Devils and Demons or other negatively charged deities. Once a person chooses to develop an immense interest in working with a corpse, it's only a matter of time before they're completely involved with primary evil forces. Thus, Kasso wasted no time and ultimately became infatuated with the Devil, Satanism and was involved in a group of kids that referred to themselves as the "Knights of the Black Circle." The group was linked with satanic ceremonial practices, and sacrificial slaughters of local pets and possibly stray animals.

Minimal this may appear; it got a lot worse. Without warning, Ricky invited a friend Gary and a few others, Jimmy, and Albert, to a secluded wooded area where the group surrounded a bonfire under the illusion that they would get high together. But as the night grew dimmer, the more sinister Kasso became. Finally, on June 16th, 1984, 17-year-old Ricky Kasso pounced onto Gary, stabbed him between 17 and 36 times, and gouged out his eyeballs. Ricky shouted to Gary during the horrendous attack, "Say you love Satan!" Each time Ricky demanded, Gary wept, saying, "I love my mother."

As word got out from Ricky Kasso's mouth that he willingly sacrificed Gary to Satan, what seemed like foul play quickly developed into severe suspicion. Ricky Kasso and Jimmy, 17, and Albert, 17, were soon apprehended; both Jimmy and Albert confessed to what had happened that night. Albert stated that he had taken so many hallucinogens that he couldn't comprehend what was happening and doubted if any of it was real. Though Albert didn't participate in the murder of Gary, he claimed that Jimmy did by pinning Gary down as Ricky stabbed him to death.

If that satanic killing wasn't evidencing enough, many others reached newspapers across the nation, scaring even the bravest of men to stay home and lock their doors. Charles Manson and the murderous killing cult "The Manson Family" would be among the most notorious crimes and cults in history. Charles Manson's connection and deep-rooted grooming brainwashed his elected members to partake in the brutal slayings of pregnant actress Sharon Tate and other Hollywood residents in the late 1960s. "The Family" was a group of about 100 followers of Charles Manson who shared his passion for unconventional lifestyle and usage of hallucinogenic drugs, such as magic mushrooms and LSD. The Manson family resided in a deserted ranch in the San Fernando Valley. Without question, they believed that Manson was a reincarnated Jesus Christ with prophecies of a race war and other extreme, controversial ideologies. Whatever Charles Manson told his young followers to do, especially women, they did it without question. The workings of a brainwashing demented cult guided by the tools of grooming and saturation of the human mind will do that after so many months on a drug trip. The Manson Family, including its loyal disciples, has committed around 35 killings. However, most of their cases were never tried, in part for lack of evidence.

Without enough evidence, it's hard to say whether Charles Manson himself was a devout Satanist, nor did he ever admit that he was. However, it's safe to say that it's indeed questionable and remarkably possible when taking attention to the cult itself and its evil goals through the seemingly ritualistic killings. So, to be fair, I cannot say outright that Charles Manson or The Family were Satanists, but it begs the question: if we asked them today, what would their answer be?

In defense, some may say that those murders are old and don't happen anymore. My answer would be -have you not seen the news? Have you researched to know this for sure?

Yes, many satanic killings still happen. For example, in 2020, 19-year-old Danyal Hussein was arrested for murder after stabbing Bibaa Henry, 46, and Nicole Smallman, 27, to death. Danyal had pledged to carry out a "campaign of vengeance" by killing six women every six months in a handwritten agreement with the "King Lucifuge Rofocale." Thankfully Danyal's killing spree was cut short due to accidentally cutting himself during the mindless attack on the sisters, which enabled police to track him down through his DNA.

Hussein stabbed Bibaa Henry 8 times before turning his apathy to Nicole Smallman, who suffered 28 stabbings as she courageously attempted to defend herself.

About ten days had passed until the sisters were reported missing by their worried families on the evening of June 6th, 2020. Sadly, before the police arrived, Ms. Smallman's partner Adam Stone found their lifeless bodies in the bushes. Hussein was arrested on July 1st, 2020, after the police discovered a link in his DNA and at the crime scene of the murder. The police searched Danyal's bedroom at his mother's home in southeast London. They uncovered various occult books on magick, handwritten demonic symbols (commonly known as sigils), and two devil's pacts written and signed in blood. In the first pledge, Hussein vowed to kill six women every six months to win the Mega Millions Super Jackpot, and in the second, he offered blood to a "demon queen Byleth" to make a girl at his school fall in love with him.

During his court appearance, Hussein turned his back on the judge. Detective Chief Inspector Simon Harding said, "He acted like a belligerent child. He's shown complete disrespect to the court system, turning his back on the judge, trying to stare out the family, and laugh, and sticking up loser signs," he added. "He has behaved like a teenage boy, but he has committed some of the most savage crimes we have seen for many years in one of the biggest police investigations."

Alarmingly, Hussein was diagnosed with an autism spectrum disorder. Police said Hussein had also been referred under the counter-terrorism Prevent program in October 2017 by his school, the Thomas Tallis comprehensive in Blackheath, due to concerns of displaying signs of vulnerability to radicalization, terrorism, and far-right ideologies.

Hussein's occult material findings concerning the "demon queen Byleth" rings alarm bells. Because that demon isn't a demon at all, It's a devil. Byleth isn't typically identified nor spelled as such, but as "Beleth" or "Bileth" is a Devil King mostly recognized in *The Goetia of the Lesser Key of Solomon*. Demons identified as "kings" are Devils in the demonic hierarchy. Unfortunately, Danyal wasn't pledging himself to just any demon; he had sold his soul to a devil that not only does exist but can make sure that once you make these types of promises -you keep them. Danyal's case is not uncommon and happens more than is reported in the daily news (and should be reported!). Devil's most definitely can manipulate a person under the influence of black evil magick to force hypnotism in what's commonly known as a "love spell." But it's not a love spell. Devils and demons don't do spells like the typical witch or wizard; instead, they complete the process of magick with manipulation of the energies of the victim by forcing them to be in a trance-like state. The "spells" take away the person's free will, thus enforcing the devil to make the person's wish come true.

So, could Danyal's wish be granted if he was successful? - Absolutely! However, very little does this come to pass because devils don't want humans to get their wish granted, for then they would no longer need the devil for help. So, instead, the devil continues to allow the person that sold their soul to suffer, so they can continue to feed off of that person's soul energy 'till they die and go to Hell.

Satanism is one of the most sinister threats to humanity. Like Kasso and Hussein, these boys were kids and were easily influenced by the devils to commit the worst crimes imaginable. Yet, the most frightening part that links these two cases together that even I've caught myself is both stabbed their victims many times. Coincidence? -I doubt it. Devils and demons have a particular way to highlight themselves into the lives of humans and sneak past our radar. Once they've been able to grab ahold of a person's interest, that's when they snatch you as soon as possible into believing that even the worst of crimes is worth committing, all for the sake of someone to love you or a few million dollars.

Highlighting my points, after the brutal murder of the sisters, Hussein went and bought himself over thousands of dollars worth of lottery tickets, only to have lost it all. He didn't lose that money because it failed somehow. He lost that money because devils are liars and will continue to keep you believing in their lies, to do their work that is evil and full of hate without mercy or love.

If one encounters a proclaimed Satanist person, it'd be wise not to put your trust in their judgment but your own. Satanists often lie and manipulate to get what they want, and it's been reported by Ed and Lorraine Warren through their occult workings and studies on devils and demons to proceed with great caution. Never turn your back on a Satanist, nor assume they're good intended. From over fifteen years of experience in the paranormal and psychical understanding, it's prudent to tread carefully when in the vicinity of a Satanist. Satanists are not all bad people, but that doesn't mean that the one you encounter won't be. Let us not forget that strangers are strangers and must be perceived as a possible threat to protect one's kin and themselves. It doesn't matter what a Satanist necessarily says but how they behave, act, and who or how they practice ritualistically. Each Satanist mustn't be judged on their belief system but their character and mannerisms with respect and dignity -while keeping your guard against any who may wish you harm as they smile your way.

As much as I would like to say that not all Satanists are evil - which is true, the fact of the matter is, their chosen god IS, and their demons are evil in every sense of the word spoken in as much of a whisper. So be cautious, my dear reader, for the very notion of a Satanist can bring one bad luck, curses, hexes, and even the case of a demon in your own home.

THE LUCIFERIAN

Luciferians are very similar to Satanists, but the difference is they serve and put their faith in Lucifer entirely. Lucifer is not just a fallen angel but a god-like entity with great respect for Satan, the devil. Christianity gets this part mixed up respectfully, stating Lucifer was cast out of heaven because he disobeyed God and wanted to be like God. However, though this is true, I've learned from encountering Lucifer years ago that he said that he left heaven through his own free will. Lucifer didn't like heaven and felt he was better off where humanity would praise him, topping his ego to the brim.

Meeting Lucifer will appear like a golden entity similar to a benevolent angel but don't get this confused. His appearance is glamorous but nowhere near benevolent nor in the slightest compares to true beauty. Beauty from an angel in the alignment of goodness and love will be everlasting in love, kindness, and humility. Lucifer, however, prioritizes himself on his ego, his reputation, and how he appears to women especially. His goal is to capture the eye of an earth woman to harness enough sex slaves and obedient, mindless women who cannot think for themselves. As a psychic medium, I've met many angels, including Archangel Michael and Lucifer, at the same time. When I met Michael, his energy and approach were precisely how one would expect. He reigned supreme in a glowing white light with a shine and masculine beauty I've never witnessed before in a man. He has the most incredible authority that brings security no matter where you are or what you feel. Lucifer, on the other hand, gives the exact opposite. Although he has a face of an angel and the smile of a supermodel, his energy is lower than any benevolent being I've encountered. Subordinate vibration angels, also known as **Fallen Angels,** wreak egoic narcissism and apathy before your insecurities.

Luciferians worship Lucifer without question and say so specifically without hesitation proudly. The fact remains, Lucifer is just as dangerous as any other evil entity due to his link and deep admiration for Satan. Satan and Lucifer are separate beings that are not the same. Satan managed to tempt Lucifer's ego, which led him to his downfall. Luciferians will say otherwise and will argue against this description of him defensively. Luciferians work with demons, devils, and other dark forces under the misconception it's not evil but walking in the alignment of a more powerful consciousness. This is not only a lie but a carefully constructed manipulative move from the devils to get humanity to fall for the demonic trap camouflaged as Luciferin.

Remain on your guard around those that choose this damned allegiance, for the damage can become more significant than expected. Luciferians tend to carry highly negative energy everywhere they go due to the demons and devils they chose to work within their magick or other ceremonial practices. Although they may have the biggest hearts, Luciferians tend to be naïve in the deception and cognitive manipulation of devils and demons. Devils and demons will most often become attached to the Luciferian. Upon attachment, the host is set up for more sinister energetic workings that can lead those around them to be victims of demonic attacks, unexpected accidents, depression, anxiety, paranoia, nightmares, paranormal activity, and even diabolical temptation. Like the Satanists, Luciferians are highly unreliable due to lying and manipulative maneuvers. If one chooses to be in the same room with a Luciferian -heed my warning and remain on your guard. Though they may be kind, it doesn't mean their demon or devil is.

THE DEMONOLATER

Demon Workers, also known as **Demonolatrists,** align themselves in **Demonolatry.** Demonolatry is a form of demon working where the person chooses to work with a chosen demon or a devil entity. Demonolaters are demon worshippers who most commonly state they only work with demons, not worship them. This blatant lie has been roaming the internet and the bookshelves in the occult for ages, but it has only recently become something of a socially acceptable choice of worship.

Unbeknownst to me, I wasn't aware of how many demon worshippers were watching my YouTube channel. Over time I began to receive letters from demonolaters specifically ordering me to cease all of my videos on demons, and one targeting a King Paimon video. I got so many complaints from people stating they couldn't believe how stupid I was on how little I understood demons and the devil King Paimon.

My King Paimon video I made in August 2020 exposed the devil and how it took me to hell in my sleep. King Paimon is still brutal to speak about publicly, but I made that video to expose the devils' evil and malice. Unfortunately, the demonolaters didn't believe my experience or take my story seriously. Instead, they laughed at my painful experiences and claimed I didn't meet the real King Paimon.

Not only did I meet the real King Paimon, but I also encountered him after foolishly summoning him on the astral realm. -Point made; it was a lesson learned! I didn't want to worship nor work with him but to see if these types of entities were indeed fundamental. No matter how many books or movies portray a specific spirit, I never honestly believe in their existence unless I've encountered the spirit myself. The fact is, when this encounter occurred, my whole life went to the pits. I was losing my relationships with my family with friends and suffered from a deep depression that led to thoughts of suicide.

When I came out and shared my story on my YouTube channel, I got a lot of heat from disbelievers and doubters and most definitely from demon worshippers that swore they would put a curse on me if I didn't take that video down. I received death threats, curse threats, and those stating they believed I deserved everything King Paimon did to me in hell. *"You got what you deserved,"* or they'd spat, *"That's what you get for summoning a King, you dumb bitch!"* They flooded and still flood my comment sections with large amounts of profanity full of hateful aggression. The likelihood of their mercy wasn't possible and remained to rain on my victory of surviving a devil-like King Paimon.

One demonolater took it personally, so; she went to the lengths of sending me hate mail. Her public name is out in the open, but we will call her *"Demon Kandy"* in this book. Though I didn't think much of it, I found a few letters from her alarmingly concerning. In one letter, in particular, she called my daughter a *"bastard kid"* and threatened to send a curse on her and me if I didn't take the video down. I was so appalled by this that I took it upon myself to look her up online to do some investigating. Not only did I find her own YouTube channel in the exact likeness of her attitude, but I found she had a video that is now deleted where she showcased her cell phone, and the wallpaper was of King Paimon's demonic sigil. The second I saw this, I knew she wasn't just any hater. "Demon Kandy" was a devout King Paimon worshipper. It changed the whole ball game to a far sinister enemy.

About a few weeks had passed when I didn't get any more emails from her, which I thought was good. Unfortunately, she was on the prowl to send me one of the worst *"gifts"* I could've ever imagined... and that "gift" was a **devil.** It was on a night that I wasn't feeling like myself. I was more impatient with everything in the household and just seemed angry at the things I usually wouldn't be so upset over. The moment I laid down to sleep was when I suddenly found myself forced onto the astral realm, stuck in a sleep paralysis state. I was unable to move my body or my astral body. The moment this happened, I felt a strong presence standing next to me on my left, and to my utter disbelief, it was a bright red figure standing next to my bed right in front of my window. The figure was so bright red I could hardly believe what I was seeing. The singular force of this entity appeared masculine and human, wearing a hat on his head that concealed most of his face. And though I couldn't make out his facial features, I was pained by the sight of his long-ass fingernails that would be mistaken as claws. The claws must've been at least 8 to 12 inches long, following with a sinister grin that was highlighted from his sharp teeth. After several seconds, I knew this wasn't a typical demon but a devil, which prompted several attempts to plead for Archangels to rescue me. No matter how many times I tried to contact them telepathically, however, it didn't seem to work.

As the entity walked towards me, he began to speak inside my head. I could hear his voice that almost sounded pleasing, but I knew better. I knew this entity was a deceiver and an ancient one at that. But as I tried to break free from this paralysis hold, it began to stroke my legs with his sharp claws. I begged him to let me go but instead, he and other demons started to assault me sexually. When that wasn't enough, the next thing I know, my body began to shake uncontrollably in demonic possession by the devil himself. During the possession, I felt enormous amounts of physical pain. The devil forced my body not only to move up and down violently, not too soon; I was levitating in the air. The devil wasn't alone; many other demons and minions were with him. During the attack, I also heard a woman's voice that sounded very familiar cackling in the background, which told me she was a witness to this horrendous and humiliating assault.

-

To know how to protect, is to understand the measures as to why. Demons and Devils are the worst enemy humans will ever face. No human is untouchable to the devil's grasp and must be vigilant in recognizing the dangers that may very well appear in your room without warning! This story and others like it are not intended to send you to fear or engage in negative energies like them. Instead, this is to educate and realize the spiritual warfare at its prime and how you can defeat it even when you're the most vulnerable.

Thankfully after what felt like minutes of one of the most painful spiritual warfare experiences of my life, I was rescued by Archangels Michael, Gabriel, and many others that I don't know. Many angels will come to our rescue when they hear our call. Even though they couldn't hear my call initially, one of my spirit guides, who witnessed the attack, could get help asap. I'm eternally grateful to my spirit guides, and we will indeed talk about how spirit guides will help you in the following pages.

When the angels arrived, I was able to be cleansed of the devil's energy as they gently massaged my arms and legs on the astral realm, as an energy therapy intended to cleanse the astral body and the soul from the toxicity of devils and other negative energy. I was so embarrassed by the whole thing. I could barely look at any of the angels, especially Michael, but even he gave me the warmest hug while saying none of this was my fault. Guilt is one of the worst enemies of the human consciousness, and the devil plays on our guilt for pleasure. Without love, we cannot defeat that which is not only a lie but a manipulated position that most often forces humans to remain unable to trust anyone or even angels. Without love and trust in the faith of the benevolence in those that carry love, we will forever be defeated. Thankfully after weeks of healing and months of cleansing by surrounding myself in only positive energy and positive spirits, I no longer identified as a victim but as a survivor.

What "Demon Kandy" did was disgusting. The sickening part is she took glee in the fact the entire situation mortified me. However, after months of healing through deep-rooted meditations and ascension on an evolved scale, my love for her has grown. I don't hate "Demon Kandy"; I only pity her lack of perception to see past the deception. She's not just a lost soul but a doomed one that will suffer at a high cost the moment she departs from the physical realm. Death isn't always freedom for the human. Depending on the god you choose, or even if it's you, you're either destined for a good place or a bad one. It all depends on your heart chakra and where your soul truly lies in the universal balance of all that is energy and truth.

    The letters "Demon Kandy" sent me...

just submitted your form: Contact on lastfrontiermedium

Message Details:

Name:

Email:

Company: -

Position: -

Subject: An explanation...

Type Here: Did you enjoy my little present? Guess what? It doesn't end with one demonic attack I put a curse on you. Paimon will not be slandered by you. Take back what you said about him and demons.

Reply to this email directly or via your site's Inbox:

Respond Now

Message Details:

Name:

Email: ▓▓▓▓▓@gmail.com

Company: -

Position: -

Subject: Why havent you taken the video down?

Type Here: Do I have to put a curse on you and your bastard kid? Take your king paimon video down NOW. He doesn't appreciate your lies. And remove your videos about me or I will report your channel for copyright and take you off of youtube. Who do you think you by the way? You're nothing but an ugly white ass bimbo who's way in over her head. Stop being lazy and get a real job instead of wasting people's time.

Reply to this email directly or via your site's Inbox:

Respond Now

3 days ago
Youre not a witch at all.

👍 👎 ❤️   REPLY

3 days ago
You know what???

From one witch to another, I'm gonna send you a present 😇 Get ready to receive 🙌

3 days ago
@Last Frontier Medium Lol I work with demons honey.
You clearly don't know what you're talking about or what you're doing, hence why you got burned by an imposter spirit and serves your naive ass right.

"Demon Kandy" and thousands if not millions of others like her are under the misinterpretation that demons and devils are misunderstood entities. A highly spoken naivety among the demon worshipper leagues highlights their ignorance. Fallen into the lie, devils will have their backs in love, support, and even close companionship. The significant issue here is demons and devils are incapable of love. These vicious monsters can't understand love, nor will they give the human the emotions that come with it. Devils, however, are highly capable of providing one the illusion of such sentiment, but this is false. The feelings are only yours being highlighted and used against you, giving the wrong impression of love from the devil, but it's all a front. None of the "loving" feelings a person receives from devils or demons is real. It's not only your emotions but also amplified to give the human target a false validation where there is none, only another illusion.

Demonolaters working closely with devils and demons are on the highest level of caution depending upon the individual's ritualistic background. None are the same but still carry a hateful energetic vibration that consists primarily of baneful, negative emotions fueled by the devil and demons they work alongside. It's not uncommon for a Demonolater to say, *"I don't worship demons, I only work with them."* -but this is a lie. Even if the Demonolater believes this wholeheartedly, that's not what the situation is. Demonolaters were tricked into this modern-aged narrative that stemmed only from more and more manipulation and lies. Demonolaters claim they don't worship demons, only work with them. And though speak this with absolute certainty, you will find that most Demonolaters have places of worship where the demon or devil's sigil is placed much like an altar.

These are the types of inconsistencies one will discover the longer you're around a Demonolater.

Lastly, Demonolaters have this unspoken belief that working with demons and devils is not in the exact likeness of selling one's soul. Thus, must make it a safer transaction, creating an equal working environment between the demon worker and the entity. Heed my warning and know this -devils and demons don't work with humans without a price and an invaluable, precious price at that. Demonolaters are being lied to by the devils and demons and will try to recruit others by inflicting them with the same mentality. The manipulative narrative can appear grand, much like a positive life advancement, but it's always at a cost. This price is irreversible, and no amount of work or worship will cover that cost.

Whatever you do in your life with a demonolater is up to you respectfully. But if one were to ask me if I would sit down with a demonolater in as little as a conversation -I'd say hell no. Demonolaters are pawns for the devil. Humanoid puppets fulfill only one thing, and that's the devil's work.

BLACK MAGICK WIELDERS

Black magick is one of the worst types of psychic attacks inflicted and wielded by those in the dark craft. There are three types of magick: White, Grey, and Black.

White Magick is primarily a positive energy force used by a witch or wizard to do good. White magick is used with the karmic understanding that what one sends out will receive in return times three. White witchcraft often aligns with healing the sick, helping others, and bringing harmony in all things.

Grey Magick, also known as neutral magick, works with good or evil intentions and finds a balanced consistency that allows the witch or wizard to harmonize without karmic damage. Neutral witches have a grounded understanding that all things in life, both good and evil, light, and dark, can be used positively or negatively in a neutral sense. In respect to this universal balance of all that is energy, the witch doesn't receive karma for excellent or hostile intentions that are done based on one's judgment of what is justice -not revenge.

Black Magick is essentially negative in terms of evil, intended to commit harmful outcomes to others and dominate situations unfairly. Demons and devils harness their powers in black magick, which mainly causes a living human to become inhumane to those around them. Black magick primarily is where the black witch or wizard works with demons and devils to complete their spells, curses, hexes, and potions with the assistance of the descended realms.

Granted, every witch or wizard will have their own set of understandings in witchcraft, but that's the basics. Magick is neither good nor evil but is determined by the heart of the witch or wizard. When a caster chooses to align themselves in the dark realm of magick, they will find only hateful and aggressive means of getting whatever it is they want. Black magick casters suffer in the sense of impatience, for the ideology is to use their powers for evil with the sole intention of taking and destroying whatever they want. I wish this weren't true, but it is. And not only is this true, but it requires a great sense of awareness to become alert to the warning signs, when possible, in the presence of a dark caster.

It would be regrettable if I neglected to share one of the most famous and treasured quotes in history. In the film (and the book) *Harry Potter and The Sorcerer's Stone,* Hagrid informed the young and impressionable Harry Potter, ... *"Understand this, Harry, 'cause it's very important -not all wizards are good. Some of them go bad."* Hagrid presented Harry a pearl of occult wisdom and a cautionary tale of what happens to wizards that condemn themselves to the depths of pure evil and malice. Unfortunately, like evil people in the world, too many evil casters will laugh at your pain, much like "Demon Kandy."

When dabbling in black magick, there are places where even most dark casters won't dare tread -and that's **Necromancy.** In the typical definition of Necromancy, it's described as a way of communicating with the dead -which is true, although there is another form of territory that breeds nefarious intentions. Necromancy, as explained earlier, is primarily used as a form of magick that deals specifically with the corpses of humans and animals. A necromancer often won't even realize that's exactly what they're doing until they're completely immersed in it. It can start small, like killing an insect for the sake of one spell, but soon they begin to kill animals to even grave robbing. When I refer to the killing of life as an example of Necromancy, it must be noted that it can include murder or a sacrifice in some form or another. Not always will a sacrifice be the case, but it does align within sacrificial means for their spells to work. A necromancer typically will commit grave robbing at an abandoned graveyard or an unmarked grave they discovered and use the skeleton's remains to place at an altar for future incantations. Necromancy isn't as common as a sacrifice, but if one were to discover a skull on another's altar, it would be wise to assume where, why, and how they got it.

The gamble when diving into witchcraft or even Wicca religion is when you open yourself up to an occultist who appears positive but ultimately is revealed as another deceiver. Without question, it must be insisted upon the gravity of danger that can be in your very home with something as simple as a book.

-Of course, I'm not talking about this book. I'm referring to the many psychics and other mystic authors who write material for the education of the occult and magick. However, one may become easily conned into another demonic trap without observing the signs.

There are several authors who wrote books that had me nearly convinced just by their benevolent covers. The saying, *"don't judge a book by its cover,"* couldn't hold a more powerful position of truth in this other level of deception. I would feel a positive vibration from the beautifully crafted pages and narratives getting into the books but to my utter surprise some had a full detailed illustration of none other than the devil **Baphomet**.

Many psychics and witches refer to Baphomet as a pagan deity poised with life and goodness. Stating despite popular belief, Baphomet is not the devil but is the primary representation of the universal forces combined into one elemental figure. There are some that continued to reference interpretations of Baphomet from the famous occultist *Aleister Crowley* who was born in October 1875 and died in December 1947.

I'm not one to attempt to cancel or desecrate another mystic's hard work, but it wouldn't serve you well if I simply didn't place additional input that requires our attention to the details. Aleister Crowley was a wizard with recognizable abilities and information into magick and the occult. However, Aleister Crowley also worked with demons and devils in my psychic opinion. He is another example of how deceiving such interpretations of devils; can be to someone new in the world of magick.

To state it plainly, Baphomet isn't a deity that resonates with goodness, nor is the universal representation of all that is a force in the universal energies. Baphomet is commonly used in the Church of Satan and is heavily admired in the halls of Satanism, Demonolatry, Luciferianism and Devil Worship.

I've met Baphomet. He's one of the eviler devils I've not only encountered but have been attacked by as well. Baphomet isn't some misunderstood pagan deity like the Greek god Pan. Yes, this particular devil does indeed have hoofs and horns but never permit yourself to be fooled by these author's or Aleister Crowley's misinformation. These people are nothing different from Demonolaters who work with devils like Baphomet and rein in the temporary coin they receive in profiting from Baphomet's name in my professional opinion. It's utterly despicable just how vile these individuals can write something so misleading. Each time I read these types of authors' works, it gets under my skin. My personal and spiritual opinion is that work, like Aleister Crowley, isn't just toxic but will invite Baphomet into your home and space. The more frightening reality is there are authors who will encourage possession and to take Baphomet into your aura like one would accept energy of the universe. This information is not only inherently metaphysically dangerous but is soulfully fatal!

Some witches and psychics will also teach that each human has more than one soul. -I've been working with Angelic beings for years and have seen some of the worst kinds of levels of horror you could grossly imagine. I don't claim to know everything but one thing I definitely know after years in Hell -you only have ONE soul. Archangel Michael and many other deities have confirmed that every human has only one soul.

These "enlightened witches" often teach within the same psychic understandings but then twists it to fit their demonic narrative. Including Baphomet into their teachings flatly baffles me. It's equally exceedingly difficult to understand how the people trusting this work don't see these signs, but that's precisely how convincing the devil is when he gets another one of his puppets to do his job.

Demonic entities and devils work tirelessly with humanity, especially in the spiritual community. It's so easy to become duped into another con by these wicked agendas, and its paramount in establishing between universal truths/ understandings and precise manipulation and brainwashing. Because that's what this is. It's another form of new-age brainwashing that gives the new age a lousy name. Willfully aligning the new generation is one thing, but when you place demons into the mix, it's no longer new age -it's satanic and demonic.

It's essential to pay very close attention to what a person in the psychic and occult world is telling you, because as Hagrid said — "not all wizards are good." Some people will appear beneficial like those previously mentioned, and many others out there will lie to your face.

Listen to your divine message receiver whenever you research information involving psychic topics, the occult, or divination. Listen to your heart and listen to what your intuition tells you. Not what someone is trying to force you to believe, but what you feel is truth on the inside. It doesn't matter what I say to you; what matters is how it makes you think and feel. One's intuition is the only method in psychic abilities that make any sense to identify truth from deception.

When I purchased these books, I bought them with an open mind. After all, I thought that this is what I should read because everyone says so, but the moment they came to my home, I don't know how else to put it, but my heart and mind told me... *"This doesn't feel right."* I felt and heard this before reading some of the books. Though I gave the authors a chance, it still didn't seem benevolent; something was off. So, whenever you get this same feeling, I'd urge you to take a step back and listen to this feeling, for this is the same sense that will guide you into the path that is safe and right for you. Trust in your intuitive senses because It's there for a reason.

In truth, there are all kinds of toxic characters in this immeasurable world with infinite personalities. Never judge a person on one's appearance, but on the content of their character, nature -and in energy. The best way to test a person's power is to sense your emotional database and even physical responses. Your body works alongside your aura, much like a computer. Whatever happens to your aura, your physical temple will begin to embody and replicate the physical equivalence. For example: If you feel ill when you're around a specific person but then feel better when not around them, it would be a possible sign. Or if you begin to shake uncontrollably but you're not cold at all, this is a sign that the person or the situation you're in is exceptionally toxic. Your body is telling you to leave immediately. I know this personally from many different experiences where this exact example happened, and each time, it was correct. So, listen to your body along with your intuition, for they truly know best.

The body has nearly endless expressions in letting your sixth senses know what isn't in your best interest and what is good for you. Allow your body to guide you along with your intuition when researching the occult.

BANEFUL LOCATIONS

CHAPTER THREE

Baneful people are no laughing matter, nor should it be excused. Although it was a bit dark, and if it disturbed you, then I sincerely apologize. You were drawn to this book, hoping it will help you learn how to protect yourself from negative vibrations and even spirits. Not only is this for that purpose, but it's to enlighten your awareness on a grander scale of just how much this rabbit hole goes when diving into the realm of pure psychic threats. Not always will you be faced with dangerous or life-threatening situations, which I hope you never do. But as you go further, you'll uncover a deeper bond with energy in yourself and how powerful you are when embracing your energy from the power that lies within you.

As one grows in love and self-awareness, the more one learns where one's loyalty and heart truly lies—no one's immune to the previously stated threats. After learning even the most seemingly innocent of characters can easily be seduced by the devil's power and hostile forces, it's time we embark where these types of negative influences occur. The number of locations is truly endless, but to not overwhelm you, I decided to break it down to a select few that are the most toxic and harmful to one's source of positive energy.

NEGATIVE RESIDUAL ENERGY

Energy can leave an energetic mark on the land and locations one visits. When a person harbors enough negative energy, their negative vibes will trail with them and begin to seep into the energy of the exact place they are standing. The negatively charged person can muster up some of the worst energy if left at home long enough without a cleansing. The energy within the person's aura morphs and easily adapts to one's emotional state and conscious thoughts. Because of this, the person's energy unknowingly leaves a mark in something minor like the seat they sit in, all the way to the land they live on, and wherever they travel. Energy not cleansed after a long time becomes what psychics call **Residual Energy.**

There are several types of residual energy, but **Negative Residual Energy** is the most concerning for the wellbeing of a living person can be exceptionally life-threatening. Energy is a lot like a memory, but instead, it's an energetic memory, full of emotions and images of the situations that happened on the land. Whether positive or negative, residual energy will affect the living and the dead. Energy isn't limited to just the physical realm. Energy is energy. Remember, you are a spirit having a human experience; thus, all the energetic workings impact you, and everything seen and unseen.

Some of the most common ways negative residual energy is created are from negative situations in vibration. Anything emotionally traumatizing to the living will make toxic vibrations that become negative residual energy. Instances like sexual assault, physical or sexual abuse, emotional abuse, criminal activity involving drugs, violence, gangs to even prostitution, sex slavery/sex trafficking, murder and even suicide, and other ranges of examples not mentioned. Whenever situations bring people to a negative state after such circumstances, it negatively impacts their emotions, thoughts, behaviors, and even faith. Emotions like depression, sadness, loneliness, hopelessness, suicidal thoughts, anger, excessive rage, and vengeful thoughts can create negative vibrations. The more these negative emotions fester and are not healed or resolved, the more prolonged and more significant the chances of negative residual energy manifest within the location or even the home. The higher the chances for negative residual energy to not be cleared or trans mutated into positive energy, the bigger the prospects for the people to live in the vicious cycle of toxic emotions that only continue to get worse.

Later, I will discuss how to heal negative energy within yourself and cleanse negative residual energy by turning it into positive energy.

HAUNTED LOCATIONS

As obvious as this section may be, it's probably one of the most important sections to Baneful Locations. There are many individuals today going to knowingly haunted locations simply for its rise. Hoping to get that spooky experience they've dreamed of facing. Unfortunately, they quickly discover it is just like in the movies and can worsen if not done extremely carefully. It seems easy, especially when we see paranormal shows. Although it seems like a walk in the park for some of the team, it's not. These brave people go to the haunted locations to become haunted in the first place, to document the haunting, collect the evidence, and determine results as professional paranormal investigators. But even as paranormal investigators (famous or not), they tend to take negative vibrations home or, worse, an entity. Some spirits don't like to be disturbed, which is why the title "haunted location" is there in the first place. Ghosts that haunt a location are for a few reasons but are often simply by their own choice.

Just like you wouldn't like someone coming to your home and disturbing you, neither do some spirits. So, get one upset enough; it very well may attach itself to you and follow you home seeking revenge.

Haunted locations listed as haunted shouldn't be messed with as modest entertainment. When approaching the landowners, they will often speak of the bond they've experienced with the spirits on the location. Not always is the experience pleasant; however, while may share a spirit that isn't so friendly and hate women or men specifically. Some sites are indeed haunted but may not be titled as haunted at all. Places like hotels, bed and breakfasts, resorts, home rentals, apartment buildings, museums, restaurants, stores, graveyards, etc., can be exceptionally haunted yet be some of the most popular places on the market. The unfortunate reality is nearly every location has at least one spirit because spirits are drawn to the living.

Whenever I'm informed that a location is haunted that I visit, my interest rises indefinitely. The haunting of ghosts doesn't typically frighten me; more so, it all depends on the type of spirits and how they haunt essentially. No haunted location is without some historical story behind it. The more one digs more profound into the location's history, empathy grows from the stories of the people and the past. It's easy to let your imagination run wild in haunting scenarios with expectations, but it's essential to keep your thoughts in check. When a spirit encounters newcomers at a haunted location, some souls like to mess with the living just to get a laugh. They like to see you scream and usually get the reaction they want, much like what we see on television. Learning to adapt to the understanding that all spirits have conscious thoughts and emotions from the history of their soul experience allows you a deeper connection to the energy, the location, and the soul.

Spirits know when your third eye is opened and will pick you out of even a group of a thousand people simply because you are more aware. You may be brighter than others, thus can attract the spirits to you more easily. When traveling to a location like this, it's one's psychic responsibility to remain calm and assertive in one's own psychic space. Don't allow a spirit to intervene in your thoughts or personal aura. Some will challenge you, while many will genuinely respect you. Nonetheless, no matter how kind a spirit may appear, never allow the spirit to attach themselves to you unless one is exceedingly advanced in how to extract that type of attachment properly.

As long as the living remains on earth, there will be haunted locations that become tourist attractions. No matter where the haunted place is, it should be taken seriously every time one approaches the area. Never let your ego get in the way and start insulting or antagonizing the spirits. Like you would appreciate respect, so do these souls that may be suffering from horrible memories from their death state or their previous life. If you decide to go to a haunted location, you take the risk of taking a chance that could lead to either a positive spiritual experience or a haunting one -literally.

DIMENSIONAL PORTALS

We live in a universe that knows no bounds. I will never claim to be an expert on everything, nor will my ego trump the paranormal department. There are still so many aspects to the supernatural that I don't know nor fully understand, but what I do know about are portals.

Portals are a level of transportation for supernatural beings that most would call alien-like beings. However, not all alien-type beings are physical entities. Shadow People, for example, are two-dimensional beings that roams within the physical and metaphysical realm. Their most known for traveling within dimensions through portals, or some may call wormholes or black holes. Portals can stay put or move from one location to another. Portals are crafted through a series of psychic abilities from the entities, which aren't entirely understood. The exploration of Shadow People is still a touchy subject due to the toxicity and danger lingering within the topic of these exceptional beings. Shadow People are shaped of human beings but aren't human in the slightest.

Portals can range in size, shape, and color. Portals can be the size of one bedroom only a few feet wide, while some portals can be as massive as an entire building. The size of a portal depends on how many spirits use the portal, how often, and what agenda. Portals consist of psychic energy, much like a mystical force. The portal can be used for multi-dimensional beings such as alien lifeforms to departed animals, human souls, demons, devils, etc. All sentient life that has a soul can travel through a portal. The purpose of portals is for entities to travel between dimensions at super-high speeds and shorten the distance. Traveling through dimensions like a portal isn't always bad when the portal is created from Angels for human protection purposes. Angels may create a temporary portal to travel between Heaven and other realms to maintain Order and protection in the universe. Although Angels do create these portals, they only last for a few minutes then dissipate the portal for human safety and others. When a portal is open for too long, it casts an unintentional invitation into our world.

The travesty in portal travel is that if a human gets caught in one, they may never get back to earth. Frighteningly enough, it's been known throughout the paranormal community that Shadow People and other dimensional beings that travel from these portals do so for human contact. Allegedly there have been reports of people vanishing out of thin air who were suspect of Shadow

People encounters. Shadow People are known to kidnap a human target and take them through these portals, never to be seen again. Not much is known as to why this is, but the video footage of Shadow People invading people's homes on the internet and published works supports this theory. The life expectancy of human retrieval or survival is close to zero. Once a human is taken into a portal, they often never return.

Portals can range in any length of longevity and distance. It can be challenging for a lone psychic medium or mystic to handle a portal by themselves. Depending on the type of portal, the human impact can be pandemonium if the human is near a portal for too long. Portals sometimes can be opened by psychic command from the host/s that manifested the portal. In essence, humans are just as capable of manifesting a portal through demonic summoning and other black magick rituals. Humans hold equal if not more powerful than other supernatural forces, which is one of the main reasons humans can also suffer long-term illnesses when in the company of a portal. Though the human psyche can withstand many adversaries, a portal conducted by black magick, demons, devils, shadow people, or negatively charged spirits can be disastrous. Portals are typically created from psychic energy that is either positive or negative. Depending on the type of energy setting the portal, it can leave lasting effects on both the living and the dead.

No matter where one goes, one may be in the vicinity of a portal. One easy way to tell is if your third eye is open, and your spirit guides notify you for your protection. Or if you're capable of identifying this on your own with astral projection or other psychic abilities. Unfortunately, not everyone is as lucky as those who have this type of guidance. The offhand is you'd be near or even living within a portal and not even be aware. The psychical and physical signs are vast, but the brief list below may enlighten your awareness of the signs when near one and what happens to the body.

PORTAL SIGNS

- Vertigo

- Headaches

- Nausea

- Nightmares of beings in your room or entities walking around in your room. These nightmares will be lucid as if the beings are physically there.

- You feel as if you're being watched.

- You feel dizzy in one particular area of the location. This type of dizziness will feel as if the room is spinning or like you're underwater.

- There is an anticipated feeling and anxiety when in the home or at the location. Sometimes you will feel a strong sense of discomfort and fear for your safety.

- Portals can allow spirits to travel through them. This being the case, if a portal was in your home, you will feel almost like a windy sensation in one area. It will feel like a swirling motion that you can't seem to shake off. Almost like you're intoxicated but sober. This sensation is due to the continual traveling of spirits going in and out of the portal.

- You experience paranormal activity. Paranormal activity can range from many things, but things moving around the home or location are the most common. For example, items moving, disappearing, and electronics turning on or off by themselves. This is because of the high amount of energy that affects the electronics and spirits messing with your things.

- Being around a portal for an extended time can significantly impact the human body, both physically and mentally. The list is nearly endless of what can happen to the person when near a portal for too long, but the most crucial effects are physical illnesses. Illnesses like a cold but then rapidly turns into the flu and something more severe that you're rushed to the hospital. Most portals themselves don't cause the illnesses; it's the low vibrational spirits that carry an immense load of insurmountable toxic energy that affects the living. From curable diseases to something more severe like cancers, tumors, stroke, or a heart attack can happen more often than even a doctor can medically explain. Some examples are other threats like mental illness that can take over, like schizophrenia, bipolar disorder, and ultimately losing one's mind.

- You may experience dreams of seeing a portal in your home or somewhere close to where you live. These dreams will be extremely lucid to the point it feels like you were wide awake.

If you ever feel as if you're possibly on the threshold of a portal, it's important to never panic during these types of pandemics. It's often sealable and can be handled by the help of an experienced Psychic Medium, Shaman, Witch, Wizard, or other ascended deities like Angels, Gods, and Goddesses that you trust. Unfortunately, not so common are priests accustomed to portals. Still, if you're fortunate enough to find one that is, it's advisable to trust in their educated and experienced knowledge in sealing the portal.

Depending on the size and the type of portal, some may not be sealed nor cleansed closed. If this ends up being the case and your paranormal advisor that you trust insists you leave the residence, it would be based on your judgment to make that life-altering decision. The threat of a portal can be fatally harmful if not taken with extreme precautions. I've come across a few portals, and each time I encountered them with my spirit guides, they instructed me it was safer to leave the location than to take it upon myself. This wasn't because I couldn't close it, or they couldn't close it. It was due to the number of spirits using the portal, much like transportation. When that transportation is favored, it's complicated and nearly impossible to stop its supernatural infrastructure. So, to spare yourself and those you love, it's sometimes best to part ways from the location and live in harmony elsewhere if possible.

OCCULT SHOPS

Mistakenly the public tends to assume the worst of people into the occult. Claiming those in the occult are all devil or demon worshippers who sold their souls in hopes of getting ahead in life. Thankfully this isn't true when that same person who believes this enters a new age store. Most new age stores possess precious positive energy that allows even the most skeptical of characters to feel a sense of welcome upon entry. I, for one, appreciate the assortments of crystals and the endless supply of white sage. Depending on the new age store and the type of owner who runs the shop, you'll encounter all kinds of positive energy. If lucky enough, you'll be gifted with this benevolent synergy, but not always are we so fortunate.

It's advisable to remain cautious whenever exploring new boutiques that target the occult and divination. New age stores generally are cheerful shops intended to provide Psychic Mediums and other mystics with an array of items like crystals, healing herbs, books, tarot cards, oracle cards, wands, cauldrons, candles, etc. New age shops and the owners have a strict policy in banishing negative energy and restricting the possibility of any negative energy entering their space. However, though most shops give the impression of optimistic intentions, the further one roams into a particular store, you may just come face to face with evil.

A few months ago, someone I once knew named Bruce and his boyfriend Andre, decided to check out a new age shop. They wanted to explore around and found one in particular. When they arrived at the location, they didn't think anything of it at first, but when Bruce's foot entered the building, he began experiencing severe dizziness. He got so dizzy he had to pace himself a few moments before proceeding. He also began receiving painful headaches that felt as if he was being stabbed in the skull without warning. His immediate impression upon entering wasn't so positive. He said the vibe in that place was so bad that he got nauseous. After only a few minutes inside, he thought he was going to vomit right there in the store. Andre got concerned, but Bruce insisted they stay to check out the store. After stabilizing himself for probably the third time, Bruce came face to face with a dark altar of candles, herbs, and a very large demonic sigil dedicated to King Paimon. When Bruce caught sight of the altar, it was clear why he was experiencing the symptoms. When Bruce and his boyfriend observed the altar in the middle of the store, they were interrupted by an angry store owner and were told to leave. Bruce explained that the store owner nearly shoved him and Andre out of the store without explanation. The woman that approached them was essentially ballistic. They both were almost frightened at her unprovoked reaction and were left baffled. This never happened to him before, and thankfully not since.

Like many other witches and warlocks, Bruce excelled in psychic abilities that tell when danger is near. The headaches, dizziness, and nausea are some of the few but most common signs when in the presence of a demon or a devil. The frightening part is the store seemed optimistic at first. He never got the impression from the outside that it would be a hostile atmosphere. He most certainly didn't expect to find himself standing within the confinement of a devil worshipper's altar and space, either.

Understand this -Demons and Devils are easily influential entities that tend to take on the form of a benevolent guide. When people begin to trust devils enough to create altars in their honor, their mannerisms start to change and not for the better drastically. This is the reason the occult gets such a bad rep. Bruce, and his beloved experienced the reaction not from the store owner but from the volatile influence of the devil she was worshipping. Devils like King Paimon have the power to take over the human host and manipulate their behavior in such a way that isn't normal. Bruce described her behavior to be bizarre and eerie. Her actions toward them were aggressive and irrational. They felt they even had to defend themselves against this woman because of how angry she was in her store. But why was she so angry?

Devils and demons know our person. They know what we are capable of and see the craft we conduct and don't. They know everything there is to know about us and then use this knowledge against us. Devils are capable of reading into your darkest desires and using them to their advantage to take control of you and those you love. And because Bruce is a loyal fan of my Lightwarrior work, the devil didn't want him or his boyfriend there. Bruce a Lightwarrior himself, sensed something wasn't right the moment he felt the psychic sting. Devils take what we do very seriously, as they should because when my viewers or I encounter evil, we *don't* tolerate it.

Bruce's experience is just a taste of what one can encounter in a demonic occult shop if not careful. Of course, this wasn't Bruce's or his boyfriend's fault. They did nothing wrong and are not held responsible. If anything, I applaud him for standing his ground and taking it like a Lightwarrior. He handled this well. It's never easy to face some of the worst kinds of devils. Bruce could also see the devil in his third eye coming out of a portal near the altar. His intuition and third eye were correct. The moment I astral projected, I saw exactly what he described. There indeed was and remains a portal in that shop, and I pity anyone who ends up being their next victim. Demons and Devils open portals whenever another human pawn creates an altar in their name. When a devil or demonic altar is erected, the devil and his minions will make their mark on the land in that space and will remain there nearly forever unless the altar is destroyed, and the area is cleansed.

If you ever enter an occult store or find yourself stumbling upon one online, be on your guard! You never know who is behind the intentions of that store or why they created it in the first place. Thankfully, there aren't many devilish occult shops, but if you do find yourself standing next to or in one, my advice is to get out of there. Distance yourself from that location at least twenty to fifty feet if possible. Demons and Devils don't take your presence lightly, and neither do those who worship them. If this comes to be your situation, don't panic. Remain in your golden white light of protection. Remain vigilant in standing in a concrete conviction of your defense and then ask your spirit guides and Angels to protect you as you leave. This is exceptionally important to ensure that no entity like a demon or a devil follows you home.

THE NARCISSISTIC INFLUENCER

Though this may seem unnecessary and even unprofessional, new age influencers are a large portion of importance to this chapter. In addition, many established influences have YouTube channels and other places where they host seminars that quickly affect impressionable people desperately seeking enlightenment.

Personally, most new agers never sit right with me if I'm being candid. Maybe it's just me. But, on the other hand, there have been several people that have shared the same experience. When I realized I wasn't alone in this, I began to dig more into the new age and those that teach in the spiritual community. With nearly twenty years of paranormal experience and observing through my years of research in the new age, demonology, the occult, and divination, I've uncovered that many new agers tend to possess narcissistic tendencies and personalities.

It's taught within the new age community in books, the internet, and within thousands of mindful groups that it's because of you no matter what happens in your life. This is a significant problem. I have a massive issue with this, for that's not the case based on the universal laws. New agers have forgotten the fundamental elements of all things in situations, people, and circumstances that make up what happens to us. If one believes everything happens because of us, then that would mean we are eternally responsible for every tiny and significant thing that happens in our lives and others that we interact with. It's such a deplorable suggestion that it would mean that even children that are murdered, that it's because of them. Like when a little girl is kidnapped, raped, and murdered -it's because her energy or her thoughts weren't positive enough, thus creating her destruction. It would mean that Bruce and his boyfriend attracted this woman to attack them head-on without a reliable explanation.

When I use child victims in a debate against a new ager, they're left speechless. Like most would see, they know that one cannot blame the child in that scenario because that would be insensitive to the victims and inhumane. It would be despicable to blame the victim in that type of situation, but unfortunately, many believe in this adamantly.

New agers are not all bad people. I, for one, have a fondness for those in the new age, but that fondness often isn't reciprocated. Nonetheless, there's more to life than just ourselves in the realm of energy and the law of attraction. Every person on this planet has a plan, dreams, goals, and personality that perpetuate what they will do today and tomorrow. No matter how much a new ager spits the law of attraction as cause for nearly everything, the lower their awareness grows in remembering this cosmic truth. We all carry our consciousness and shed our kind of energy, and it doesn't matter if you agree or disagree because it's a fact regardless. Just like the man who killed that little girl had his power and plan, so do people who wish to see justice for her death. Each piece of us holds darkness and light. And it's up to us how we choose to associate with that balance.

Without darkness, there would be no light, and without light, we wouldn't be able to recognize darkness. Darkness is not to be identified as evil. When the sun goes down, and the moon rises, we don't associate the moon with the devil. Instead, we gaze at its brightness in the night sky and gleam in our imagination. Accepting the darkness within the universe, we can accept the world's harshness and ourselves. It's to be known the embodiment of the soul is neither good nor evil. It's in one's conscience that creates the monster or the savior.

If you identify yourself as a new ager, I don't assume this of you automatically, nor is it wise. This is commonplace with most new agers who struggle with accepting cosmic realities. A lot of New agers as a whole wish to bring goodness back into the world. That's what drew me towards Lightwork and being in unison within the spiritual community. But the deeper I dove into myself as a spiritual being having a human experience; the more revelations hit my awareness like a lightning bolt. Every spiritual concept has its pros and cons, and the new age teachings neglect to accept the scam outside of themselves. In essence, the new age teaches that we can control everything by simply changing how we think. Though much of our life circumstances can most definitely be altered and adjusted with mindfulness, we cannot merely control everything.

Not all new agers think alike. Most tend to bend and twist things to fit their iconic narrative that may not mold well with others. For example, the new ager that speaks of chakras and crystals may be crude, rude, and cold simply because you may disagree with one thing. This happens a lot, believe it or not. When I entered the new age world, I thought that all new agers were kind, gentle, and generous people, but I was far too ignorant. New agers can be mean, cruel, and hateful people just as much as a Satanist or an atheist. Not to mention the use of labels like these tend to separate people, which is not that far from other religions. New age truly is a cult in itself in many instances, given enough power, money, and permission to take over the minds of millions of people with enough manipulation.

The new age isn't untouchable to manipulative narcissists. There are noteworthy famous influencers and spiritual speakers known for arranging their followers to eat a certain way, act a certain way and never question their motives or even question themselves. Whenever a person claims or behaves as if they are the walking messiah, it's been recorded throughout history that these "enlightened" people tend to manage catastrophic ends. In worst case scenarios, some are notorious for teaching the public that suicide is not harmful against oneself; instead, it is a "restart button". Tragically, several of the followers of these teachers believed in this so much that many of these victims lost their lives to suicide.

If that wasn't disturbing enough, I've witnessed several influencers insinuate that demonic spirits are parasite-like entities and are merely the shadow aspects of yourself. Claiming that people that aren't adequately healed from their past trauma etc., in turn, subjects the person to what appears to be demonic spirit hauntings but is only an expression of your subconscious or unconscious mind calling out for help or even love. Some of these people encourage you to welcome the demon or devil into your aurific field and to love the "shadow self." These spiritual gurus have been blinding the public on a global scale to believe that the devil is a part of your shadow self and is, in fact, a part of you! -I wish I were kidding, but these people are teaching this, and the more shocking part is people are actually being convinced of this. I don't know what's worse, a person teaching this or that people are blind enough to actually believe this crap.

In simple terms, the **Shadow Self** identifies parts of the subconscious and unconscious pains that have yet to be healed within a person. The essence of the shadow self does hold some truths but has equally been over-used and extended past the notion of common sense. The shadow self is merely an aspect of one's emotions that have yet to be healed, but that doesn't and shouldn't be identified as the living person's consciousness taking metaphysical form. This is yet another form of victim-blaming.

Whenever I've made it a point to call out this diabolical narrative in the occult community, I've been accused by countless witches that I was not only ignorant and jealous of these people but was only speaking from my shadow self. Yet, I not only struck a chord but have left a mark on what most witches have been reluctant to expose in fear of the same social damage. I, for one, have no issue calling bs for what it is, and this is probably one of the more insane demonic lies. But whatever happened to just plain common sense? -In fairness, most witches I've encountered don't want to believe in the evil on the other side. Some have expressed they simply don't believe it, even though there are plenty of vile evil people on earth, yet they have a hard time grasping the innate otherworldly reality and its pure wickedness.

Another widespread misconception is the belief in Soul Dualism. This is commonly understood in Finnish Paganism, Inuit groups, Chinese cultural religions, and others dating back centuries. The popular belief in soul dualism is a person possesses up to three, even as many as six souls that are either in harmony or in conflict with one another. Some believe the souls are positioned in several body parts such as the liver, heart, and abdomen. Some even think that each chakra is the souls suggested. A virtuous person, for example, is said to be in complete harmony with their souls, whereas an evil person is continually combating within themselves. The "free soul" or higher self is said to leave the body and journey to the spirit realm during sleep, trance states, death, and insanity. Soul duality is also seen in Austronesian shamans, where illnesses are regarded as "soul loss," and to heal, one must "return" the "free soul" (which may have been stolen by an evil spirit or got lost during astral projection in the spirit realm) into the body.

I'll never state I know everything. However, by the advisory by my Spirit Guides, they've said that, just like most of what is described in the Holy Bible isn't true, so is this. I can adamantly tell you that most human beings have only one soul. I say "most" because there are, in fact, exceptionally evolved people that reincarnate with their twin flame and join together into one human body to help humanity. This is relatively similar but is uniquely rare and exceedingly complex. Can a person's astral body be kidnapped and taken to another realm within the dimensions? - Absolutely. But it's to be carefully understood that the astral body IS the soul, and the astral body is who you are and not separate from you. Nor do you possess dual souls. Dual souls are another form of separation from one's choices, medical reality, and lack of taking complete accountability.

The other main reason I know this is from personal experience when I was in Hell for over 1800 years. When I was there, I was not in control of anything that occurred, nor could I manipulate the dimensional experience -which most believe would be capable of giving it's created from your Shadow self. The misguided belief of Hell is that when a person experiences a Hell that it's not an actual realm but is the subject of your Shadow Self. But I can tell you from personal experience that's severely untrue. When one is in a realm, you cannot control the entities or the actual dimension itself. You have **NO** control. During the torture I endured in Hell, I could not feel, sense, see or identify even close to the relative idea of being a soul that was separated from my other souls. Everything I endured was pure to my being that was of the only one soul we possess. To add, if an astral body were to be kidnapped and taken to another realm, this absolutely can cause a person to lose their mind towards insanity, even physical immobility, and even go into a coma. However, the person's astral body is still attached to their physical body, thus causing the living person twice the suffering.

A person only possesses one soul as the human body only needs one soul. So, there are indeed several spirits (souls) combined into one person, but most psychics understand this to be an actual possession of evil spirits. Evil spirits want the human race to believe that you have multiple souls, so they won't be faced with the threat of an exorcism which has also been understood by the instruction of my highly ascended Spirit Guides. Soul dualism is only relative to less than 1% of people on planet earth, and even then, it's a temporary engagement with other spirits, and then quickly they depart. Lastly, when a person dies and becomes an earth-bound spirit, that soul stays on the earth realm by choice. No soul is left behind by their "other souls" or even left by the Higher self. Again, I've encountered many spirits and have been instructed countless times by Yehoshua (Jesus Christ) and many other benevolent spirits that humans only have one soul, period.

Those who teach that people possess multiple souls and then attempt to entice their followers with the idea that even Baphomet is merely a philosophical representation of the universe and of you, or that devils are benevolent are people bound by deception and demonic manipulation.

One of the best and worst lies ever told was that the devil doesn't exist. It shouldn't be surprising that witches are given such a bad rep due to this demonic narrative that even most witches themselves are blind to seeing. It's not unusual for witches not to see eye-to-eye when it comes to magick, the occult, and countless other subjects. But for even witches themselves to not be challenged to see this devilish tactic again leaves me stunned. How can one not see the lies and manipulation right before you? How can you become convinced that even devils or demons are merely the shadow of yourself? -Do you like this lie? Do you genuinely believe this is true, or were you peer pressured to think this because someone told you to?

I've learned from *Archangel Michael* and many ancient *Egyptian Gods like Isis, Osiris, Thoth,* and even the late Ed Warren that devils manipulated their existence to blend within the darkness of the human guilt and the subconscious. Everyone has a dark side. No one is perfect, and devils knows this very well. What better way to make you believe you're responsible for the Demonic haunting than by insinuating it was you all along. With this in mind, one cannot help but find this to be grotesquely genius that even the devil himself made you believe you were a part of him and he's a part of you. Without seeing a conscious separation or a clear metaphysical conclusion, this would ignite many people to blame not only themselves but begin accepting the devil and demon soulfully. Again, putting plainly, this is *precisely what the devil wants.*

When I started my YouTube channel, I got a lot of hate from people telling me I would never be like some enlightened teachers. Some of them shouted obscenities telling me I was a copycat and wouldn't even fit in the spiritual community. For a long while, I would let it go, but after a few months, I couldn't take it anymore and began a google search on some of these people that I was being compared to (I was compared to many!). Upon my research I began to learn more about the impact of these teachings. People were being brainwashed much like a clan to slam anyone who they think is remotely relative to their messiah.

Many narcissistic teachers in the spiritual community take it upon themselves to extend a hand of enlightenment when it's a way to make you worship the ground they walk on. Many folks accuse me of the same thing, which is laughable. I, for one, don't like the idea of people worshipping me. It's creepy! Narcissists like the idea of all eyes on them and everyone groveling at their feet when they enter a room. That's the messiah mentality hidden by their narcissistic personality in search of receiving acceptance and admiration.

What I teach is drastically different. I don't believe people will see the truth in me. I never and will never teach this because that's not true. Discovery of eternal truth is through personal self-discovery in meditation and help from one's spirit guides. Yes, I often state that I've reached an ascended level in meditation and have excelled in Lightwarriorship, but I will never announce to anyone that you cannot get there yourself.

Last but certainly not least, I don't tell my followers nor my viewers that suicide is a "restart button" because it's not. Any genuine Psychic Medium and an enlightened individual would know that suicide is gravely discouraged for it's the ultimate loveless act upon thyself. Angels and Starseeds (celestial beings) relay the emotional and mental damage caused by suicide and should be prevented as much as possible. Suicide stops the soul from advancing in their earthly incarnation, for living on earth hastens the learning curve and soulful ascension faster than when on the other side. Someone so enlightened should know this, instead insists this on their followers while also claiming those committing suicide have reincarnated the very next day. As a psychic medium who knows the dead well, I was truly disturbed by this exaggerated and psychic lie. All genuine psychic mediums know that it typically takes a departed soul years to centuries to reincarnate for soulful ascension reasons based on lessons learned.

Narcissistic people take great advantage of the spiritual community because it's the best place to receive what they want. It's the perfect place to take the rein, use their ego, and make it appear they can walk on water. If you're ever in the presence or discover a YouTube channel, blog, books, or other forms of material as described, it's encouraged to take the matter into your intuitive judgment. Take time to investigate. Listen to your intuition by allowing your feelings to guide you to decide for yourself. Just because someone has a lot of followers, doesn't mean what they teach is authentic, correct, loving, or logical.

SATANIC TEMPLES & ALTARS

Did you ever notice that even Christian churches have altars dedicated to their God? As ironic as this is, most Christians don't realize they too have an altar dedicated to their benevolent God, and there is no shame in that. Whatever one does that is harnessed and done in love and honor for your chosen God is harmless, as long as it remains to be benign. However, there are many places one may go and discover you landed at a location dedicated to the not so friendly of Gods and entities.

Altars are essentially a table, desk, and sometimes set up on the floor with candles, herbs, pictures, statues, flowers, and other things to represent the entity the altar is for. Not always are altars done in a public place. Still, every so often, there will be that devout demon worshipper or worker that will set up an altar outside in a cave, a beach, or somewhere deep into the woods to conduct ceremonies and sacrifices. It's been widely known that many satanic altars are done underground in sewers or abandoned homes and buildings. Often one may discover blood and an animal carcass not that far from the altar. It's a tragedy when it happens, for an animal's life is so precious. A life taken is a life not spared. Animals and even humans sacrificed in these rituals will open a doorway to Hell, branding the location as Hell's doorway. It's known by paranormal investigators like *Zak Bagans* from *Ghost Adventures* that during his investigations, the energy on the land was so tarnished that you can feel it within your very skin. Not always will one encounter an altar-like Zak or Bruce, but you will feel the energy affect you almost immediately when and if you do.

Whenever an altar is erected for devil or demon worship, it causes the energy within the entire area to become tainted. Witches that conduct black magick to curse or harm another with the help of devils or demons will leave hazardous energy. No longer are you dealing with simple negative residual energy. Instead, you're dealing with Hell's realm. Portals to Hell can be manifested from these kinds of altars, and once they're opened, it's nearly impossible to close them yourself. This would require many excellent Archangels, other Angels, and other ascended beings to close a portal to Hell. The portal itself is always guarded by demons and devils and is continually used to maintain that negative charge on the land. The more this negative charge has fluctuated, the greater the chances of influencing more humans to do the devil's work.

You must *never* touch anything on the altar if you ever come into contact with an altar like this. These altars carry immense energy that has the same potential to curse you the moment you touch the items. This same rule applies to other altars made by witchdoctors that focus on hoodoo or vodou. The best move would be to step away from the altar and leave as far away from that location as possible. Never take anything home from the altar -not even a rock! It doesn't matter what you found; leave it there and if you discover any sacrificial evidence, report it to your local police or security.

After departing from the altar, you may discover that you endure a series of horrific images, thoughts, and even nightmares. These are other forms of psychic attacks. If you're experienced, you'd know how to quickly cleanse yourself through several mystic measures to stop the psychic attacks. However, if you're seeking guidance and tips, I provide answers to how to cleanse yourself and stop the psychic attacks before they start in *Chapter Eight: High Defense and Purification page 213.*

CURSED LAND

Cursed land is probably one of the trickiest of psychic attacks and has the potential to cause harm in nearly every way imaginable. There are several ways to identify cursed land, but not always will it speak to your psychic senses right away. Sometimes it may take time to identify the curse and comprehend its toxicity.

Cursed land isn't created by itself. Cursed land happens when a human being or a spirit decides the ground is theirs and sends a hateful evil charge of powerful energy into the land itself. This energy is often crafted by some type of witchcraft and a magick that attaches itself to anyone that touches the ground or sometimes just remains on the land. Not always is cursed land going to follow a person to another location. Often, the cursed land will be just the land itself, and once the person leaves, they are no longer affected by the curse. Unfortunately, there are curses strong enough to seep into the trees, plants, and buildings built on the land. A home built on Native American land that has been cursed, that family will endure intense amounts of haunting experiences like nightmares, daymares, paranormal activity and have terrible luck with their health, finances, relationships, and practically everything else. Native American cultures in the distant years and still today take their spiritual beliefs to heart. Some of the most profound and powerful curses are created by Native Americans from centuries ago.

Spirits can take control of a chosen space and feed on that land and anyone and anything on it. Lower vibrational spirits are psychic parasites that suck all of the light from positive living people to continue to gather power to harm others further. It's not necessary to take energy from others, but psychic vampires like lower vibrational spirits will take what they want due to their egocentric greed. Lower vibrational spirits like earth-bound souls and demons are best known for taking over homes, land, and people because of senseless hate. This hate festers from within the soul of the being that lashes out, using it against others without mercy. At times this hate can turn into an unintentional curse that carries on for centuries in the family home to even the unaware victims.

There are other yet rare occasions where nature and natural elements will create their curse to protect the land. **Elemental Entities** are not widely known even within the occult community, nor is it often spoken through the common tongue. Elemental Entities are typically harmless when the human race respects the earth with tender care. However, there are Elemental Entities that will take it upon themselves in a war against humanity to protect the land and the livelihood of animals. Earth, air, fire, and water are the types of Elemental Entities' typical appearance to the likeness of nature. The best way to avoid confrontations with Elemental Entities is to do the best you can to respect the nature of the earth and all that lives on it. Elemental Entities come in all shapes and sizes and will protect their land at all costs. Granted, it may appear with forest fires occurring that they aren't doing a good job. But, on the contrary, elemental Entities will seek justice for the chaos that arises in mysterious ways without ever being the wiser.

Whenever one goes camping or something as small as picking a flower from the ground, it gives thanks to nature for its beauty and livelihood. Repaying the earth by planting flowers, trees or simply doing your part by picking up trash in your town are some of the many ways to pay our respects. I've been graced to meet several Elemental entities, and they are some of the wisest and kindest of beings. They ask we respect their home as much as we would appreciate the same in ours.

Coming into contact with a curse can do insurmountable damage to the human being and the soul. If you feel you're living on cursed land or know someone, it's best to seek professional spiritual help to resolve the issue. Unfortunately, not all psychic mediums, witches, and warlocks will know how to dismantle a curse. Sometimes one may face the odds that it's impossible to be rid of the curse due to its complexity and the caster that manifested it. It's commonly believed that once a curse is cast, it's impossible to prevent, but you'll be relieved to know this is also untrue. Curses and hexes can be contained even if a Black Magick caster sent them. What would be required are a wide range of exceptionally ascended beings like Angels and psychics to stop the curse in its tracks. This also includes in generational curses. No matter the type of curse, it can be eliminated with the right power and a loving force.

HOME

Meeting face to face with evil can sometimes come to us by surprise, in the least likely of places. Spirits have a way of covering a lot of ground on the earth realm thus have this insatiable habit of invading our space as often as possible. Some spirits don't respect your privacy or any sense of boundaries, which is often why people share they feel invaded by something they can't see, but sense is near. Sometimes one doesn't have to guess if a spirit is among you, for the very presence of certain spirits can be so overwhelming it feels as if a living person is sitting right next to you. It's not so uncommon, yet it's rarely shared among adults for fear of being scrutinized when suspecting a ghost is in their home.

Ghosts and other types of lower vibrational spirits tend to envy the living. Some souls want to be alive again so desperately; they will go to the lengths of invading physical space, which will feel frightening to most people. It's unnerving when I hear their stories because it's not right. No spirit should ever feel entitled to crowd a living person's personal space physically or energetically. Unfortunately, even if the living person commands their right to privacy and freedom, they still feel this and sometimes even more than before. A home invasion by a spirit is one thing but feeling violated in your sense of person circulates heavy guilt and shame on the living. Most often, the living somehow finds blame thinking it's somehow their fault, but it's not, and in this section, I will explain why.

A paranormal home invasion happens a lot more than one might suspect. An entity invading a home can be one of many reasons, but each reason typically has a diabolical agenda leaving the human unable to sway this uninvited guest. There are nearly endless ways and reasons for a spirit to find its way to your home and begin haunting your family. The list is so vast, but I've summed it down to a few of the most common ways a spirit will invade your home.

PARANORMAL HOME INVASION

- You were involved in Paranormal Investigations or work in the paranormal field.

- You stayed at a hotel, and the entity followed you home.

- Visited another haunted location like an office building, school, friend's house, store, or other potentially haunted locations.

- Used a Ouija Board, Spirit Talking Board, or a Satanic Ouija Board.

- Using Tarot Cards that involved Demons or Devils.

- Researching the paranormal, the occult. Watched satanic documentaries, movies, and shows about the supernatural.

- Have a friend that is into the occult. Know someone who is a Satanist or aligns themselves with working with dark magick and or entities.

- Came across items or other locations most known for curses with entities attached. *(We will discuss haunted things in Chapter Four: Baneful Rituals page 117)*.

- You were a part of a séance to contact the dead or another type of occult ritual involving evoking or invoking entities.

- Your third eye has opened and been roaming through the spiritual dimensions knowingly or unknowingly.

- Moved to a new home and discovered the haunting a mere few days after your arrival.

These are some of the more common reasons individuals will face a haunting. Each has its flaw and resolution, but never feel guilty for your curiosity. As Angels have instructed through my own mistakes, no person is judged on their choices through discovery but must be handled with care. Those who dive into the occult's dark aspects uncover unkind elements that usually leave them unwilling to continue down that path. However, the slightest rejection and deterring from the left-hand path can anger the spirits one may have summoned. Detaching from the dark magick is easy; it's disconnecting the entities that's a bitch. All entities within Black Magick spells, and Satanism breeds an army of foes worth even the most revolutionary of forces to undertake a beating. Regret is usual, but don't place blame in your heart. If you were curious about the left-hand path but found it's not for you, this is understandable and even better that you've discovered this truth! For no soul is meant for a life that isn't morally right.

Handling a haunting is another format that isn't necessarily typical for most psychic mediums. I'd be a liar if I said most psychics know how to banish evil. The truth of the matter is, I've come to realize more than half of them would rather smell the roses of ignorance than bear the scars of reality. Each case in my Paranormal Advisory sessions with clients has a new situation all on its own. No haunting is the same as the next, for no entity is the same as the rest. Establishing what type of entity, you're dealing with and assembling a team of experts who know how to determine the appropriate action must be done. Though I work alone in the earth realm, I have an extensive team of experienced spirits including *Ancient Egyptian God Horus* and many others who possess exceptional knowledge and benevolent godlike skill of exorcising entities and banishing negative energy for good. In later chapters I cover all there is to know about how to reclaim your space safely and securely.

Hauntings often occur when the entity has discovered something about the person they liked and decided to haunt the person. Attaching to a human is very common. A **Psychic Attachment** is when a ghost or another entity blends what seems like a cord to your astral and physical body and molds it with the living host. This attachment will feel normal at first, but then over time, the human may experience backaches, neck aches, or other sensations like a vibration on their back. This tingling feeling is not your nerves going out of whack. It's the energy vibrating in correlation with the link between you and the attached entity. Not all attachments are negative. Some attachments are done out of love and can be positive if both the human and the spirit align with loving intentions. However, this is not always the case and must be taken seriously every time. Attachments on a human host from demonic entities like demons or negatively charged human souls can be catastrophic to the human body and the soul. The longer the extension is intact, the greater the damage done to the human. Attachments happen when the entity has pointed its attention to that specific human to take its very life force. However, there is always hope, and later within the pages, we will uncover how to regain your sense of freedom from an attachment and hauntings.

Malevolent spirits that desire what they see will do whatever they can to attach themselves to it. Souls that follow a human home don't always have malicious intent. Sometimes it's merely to spend some time with the human and then leave after a few hours or even days. Not always will a spirit stay and remain in the person's life, but if this turns out to be the case, there are ways to be rid of the entity and establish a peaceful household once again.

Whether you're a Paranormal Investigator, a Psychic Medium, or even an Empath, you're bound to encounter something negative unintentionally. Every location has its sense of history and energetic vibration, where understanding those possible threats is vital. Though my outspoken opinions may appear to some as obnoxious, ignorant, or downright unprofessional -my points are validly filled with facts, nonetheless. It's not my place to gain anyone's approval in the Light Bearer community; my job is to call out the reckless psychic threats for what they are. Where there's evil, there is manipulation and frequently physical danger. Don't allow your heart's desire through the 'benefit of the doubt' take control of your intuitive alarm bells. Follow your gut regardless of popular opinion. Sometimes what is considered cool or acceptable doesn't mean it is.

BANEFUL RITUALS

CHAPTER FOUR

When coming face to face with a dark force, it's fair to ask where that sort of energy manifested and how and why. It's only natural to wonder where these sinister plots are birthed and why they were created in the first place. It's not every day an evil force will attack one, but it does and can happen when we least expect it. When our guard is down, that's when the supernatural predator strikes, leaving the vulnerable left with nothing but to beg for mercy. Something like a curse crafted in hate, revenge, or jealousy can have a sizable impact on the victim(s) targeted. Each ritualized curse or hex can leave a mark on the victim in such a way that it stays with them forever, following down the family line to even death. Those who walk in the shadows only know fear as the motivator and pain as their goal.

Before we go into the heavy details of dark rituals involving Black magick, it's essential to decipher the difference between a Hex, Curse, and Generational Curses and their potency.

Hexes

A Hex is a lighter and a temporary form of a psychic attack. Hexes are performed to cause momentary affliction but are not set in stone. Hexes can last for up to a single day to a month but typically fade over time. Hexes cause mild misery like sudden job loss, nightmares, hair loss, sudden weight gain, headaches, or fleeting moments of bad luck.

Curses

The caster designs a curse with immense hatred and vile repulsion of the victim, meant to imprison the person with intense affliction. Curses are cast to last years to even the person's timely or untimely death. Curses can be released by the caster's power alone or through the conspiration of an evil spirit. A successful curse can send the victim into a whirlwind of intense and seemingly endless bad luck, horrendous nightmares, depression, anxiety, panic attacks, migraines, sudden blindness, loss of hearing, car accidents, freak accidents, deaths of loved ones, and pets, heart attacks, strokes, cancer, unexplainable seizures to demonic oppression and possession and even death of the victim.

Generational Curses

Generational Curses are curses linked with the victim and their family line. The caster that sends this curse does so, intending to curse you, your children, grandchildren, etc. A generational curse is much more difficult to achieve depending on the wickedness and the desired outcome. Although much like a singular curse, a generational curse is functioned to cause damage to the entire family line that can even affect the extended family. Without the awareness, this type of curse will look like a simple stream of unfortunate happenings to the family. The signs of a generational curse are continuous bad luck where no matter what the family does, nothing ever seems to go right or according to plan. A cursed family always seems to lack money, security, love, empathy, and even struggle with crime, drug addiction, alcoholism, theft, abuse, paranormal activity, broken or failed relationships, unemployment, and a severe lack of hope, kindness, and faith.

BLACK MAGICK

Occult practices involving the Black Arts present a continual problem in society today. It violates the free will of its victims and permits the ones responsible with a false sense of entitlement that was never earned in the first place. Every individual is accountable for their lives and the consequences of their choices. No matter how long time has passed, the universe always keeps tabs on the deeds we do and will give us back what we have bestowed, whether we're prepared for that Karma or not. As a White Witch

Goddess, myself, I've always known this cosmic truth concerning the universal Law of Karma; however, not every Witch or Wizard reciprocates the same belief or understanding.

Black Magick carries a narcissistic agenda formulated to focus on what the caster wants. There is no conscience or guilt when Black magick is involved. All that exists in the mind of a Black magician is power, control, greed, revenge, hate, pain, and even jealousy. The Black arts have been among you more than you may realize. Though it may not be advertised to the public eye doesn't mean it isn't affecting your daily life. Those in the Black arts often wish to remain anonymous as long as their misfortunate wishes are granted against you. But just because we cannot identify them, it doesn't mean we cannot stop the curse in its tracks!

Within magick, there's an understanding that all in the universe has its unique power that is docile until it finds a purpose to be awakened. Inside every human being is a powerful God and Goddess ready to emerge and take the reins of one's power and destiny. Each moment you're in meditation, you're circulating your psychic power that enables your type of protection and even affliction. However, no amount of power can be wielded without first understanding and respecting its nature and how it is manifested.

Energy for good can heal the wounded, resolve a situation, and mend a broken heart. A power manifested in hostility leads to endless bad luck, broken dreams, broken hearts, and even death. As the saying goes, there is a level of truth that what one manifests is who they are inside. When a person chooses the path of the dark arts, they're permitting evil to take over their soul; however, most of those in this path aren't remotely aware of this. Within

Hell, for example, when a devil or a demon takes over a person in this realm, it's because they were able to dismantle the human's ability to fight back. When a soul loses the fight against evil, malice takes over that person's soul and is no longer the driver of consciousness. I know this from personal experience when I was in Hell for over 1800 years. Whether you believe my experience, it doesn't matter. What matters is the information is factual, and it's what I learned during my time there and how demons take over a human's choices. People don't just wake up one day and become black witches or wizards. It is the demonic influence that's hovered over them for years following their every move with a heavy influence and oppression. The saddest part about the black arts is that once a caster makes this decision, they simultaneously sell their soul.

The danger of Black Magick is catastrophic. Black magick can destroy everything good in a family dynamic, workplace, relationships to an entire town if truly desired and effortlessly plotted. With the help of demons and devils, the witch or wizard can take everything in their path and alter it to their desires no matter how outlandish and impossible it may seem. For example, a marriage can easily be destroyed with black magick to a family member murdered in one week. Extreme cases of black magick involved situations where people were hit by vehicles, were attacked by dogs, houses caught fire unexplainably, endless series of bad luck, rape, and people diagnosed with incurable diseases and cancers.

It's without question that the average witch and warlock within divination identify the most prominent threat are those in the black arts due to the toxicity and lack of complexity. It's relatively eerily simple when working with the forces of evil.

Aligning one's energy with an evil force like a demon or a devil requires specific rituals. Each entity requires a different set of rules when working with the spirit or requesting a favor. Working with a spirit like a demon is often taught in the occult that demons and devils will "help" the caster if one is respectful and obedient to the entity. At the spirit's request, some black magick casters will leave offerings like food, alcohol, dead animals, and even gold to gift the demon or devil. Demons and devils each possess their personalities linked to their type of requirements and regulations of offerings. None are the same as the other. For example, a demon of gluttony prefers food as an offering, whereas a demon of lust desires a sexual encounter with the caster or watches the caster during masturbation. Many dark witches perform sexual acts with their partners while knowing the demonic entity perversely observes as one of the many grotesque forms of an offering.

One must understand about demons and their likeness that just because a demon may be attracted to food doesn't mean they won't be drawn by sexual stimulation. Nor the idea of power and control won't stimulate a demon drawn by lust. Although the occult has seemingly perfected the identity of the spirits, it doesn't mean they did. I receive endless backlash from demon worshippers and those in the occult stating things like, *"this demon doesn't do that"* or *"That demon isn't drawn to those things, so you're wrong."* In sharing my horror from King Paimon, many blasted their accusations, assuming that because King Paimon isn't stimulated by lust but by other things, it wasn't Paimon who tortured me in Hell.

Let's be very clear about this. -Demons and Devils are stimulated by **EVERYTHING, AND ANYTHING** that they know will cause pain to the victim. It's instead an insult to their cognition when one takes time to think about it. They're fully capable of being intrigued by anything that's placed in front of them, no matter what or who it is. As some assume, they're not mindless puppets, nor are they unable to detach from the set of labels and identifications demonolaters and Satanists bestowed. No. Demons and Devils may be drawn to something specific like sex, food, drugs, torture, control, and alcohol, but that doesn't mean they're unadaptable. I don't say this in defense of demons or devils. I say this to enlighten one past the ideologies and labels restricting their very nature and endless capabilities.

The result is almost always the same; it's usually left with someone hurt or dead. Rituals in the black arts commonly include herbs, plants, fire, vodou dolls, cauldrons, spices to human hair, etc. The darker aspect is when it involves a blood sacrifice. Much like a spiritual currency, an animal or human sacrifice can be required when working with a demon or a devil. I don't say this portion lightly. There are millions of demons and thousands of devils, each with its own set of requirements for an acceptable offering. You'll often hear sacrifices aren't common in the black magick ritual, but this isn't necessarily the case. Statistically, the black witch or wizard will start with something harmless in the form of a sacrifice, like not eating or not doing something the caster loves. Although this can please the demon or devil for a time, it never suffices evil's hunger for death. Thus, it may not bring an adequate offering for the deal, spell, and or curse. Often when the black caster finds nothing but dissatisfaction, a morbid temptation to seek greater risk for a more successful outcome arises. As time passes and nothing seems to happen in the way the caster would prefer or expects, desperate times may come for more sinister measures.

Black magick is a form of taking away, whereas white magick is the opposite. White magick is about giving to those that cannot deliver to themselves as a form of love, compassion, empathy, healing, and mercy. Not black magick. Black magick lingers in the arms of evil lurking in the shadows of despair, waiting for the right moment to take down its target. Magick wielded by those who wish harm leads towards destruction and chaos without reason or logic. When a caster sends a curse or a psychic attack to their victim, it tends to leave breadcrumbs, meaning signs and evidence of what is considered a black magick attack. Because there are endless ways in how magick can be used, wielded, and weaponized, it's prudent to showcase a brief list of signs of black magick. It's not always the same as it will be with other casters, for each caster may use various forms of magick wielded by different forces. However, the list reveals the aftermath and side effects of psychic attacks used in black magick. Not all psychic attacks are caused by black magick, but it's far more likely to cause harm physically, mentally, energetically, and soulfully when they are.

SIGNS OF BLACK MAGICK

- Nightmares and Daymares (Daymares are nightmares from naps during daytime)

- Paranormal Activity.

- Sudden struck of illness, disease, or cancer.

- Severe depression.

- Severe suicidal thoughts and or attempts of suicide.

- Severe sudden alcohol abuse or drug abuse.

- Demonic attacks.

- Demonic nightmares.

- Devil attacks.

- Devilish nightmares.

- Astral kidnapping by a demon or a devil.

- Nightmares of the black witch or warlock attacking you, doing or saying something toxic against you and loved ones.

- Sudden struck of severe bad luck. This bad luck will seem as if nothing ever goes right, in literally everything you or your family tries to accomplish or does.

- Feeling as if you were cursed or hexed. This may repeat in your head continually in dreams, in your thoughts much like a song repeating in your mind uncontrollably. Feeling as if you're haunted by a negative energy.

- Unexplained death of your pets, farm animals or loved ones.

- Freak accidents that happen often leaving a person injured or death.

- Sexual assault, rape, incest, and molestation.

- Damage of one's reputation from lies, haters, excessive defamation in work, home etc.

- Murder, physical abuse to the family or by someone in the family.

- Repeated miscarriages or still births and death of children unexplainably.

The deeper one researches black magick, the darker and eviler it becomes. For example, a black witch like "Demon Kandy" concocted a spell that sent a few demons to my very home and the devil to attack me. If I weren't as prepared as I was, I wouldn't have known how to handle it as well as I did. Yes, it struck enough fear and pain that I had to heal from the attack for months, but it didn't do what she ultimately wanted. "Demon Kandy's" goal was to scare me away from my work, but it failed. Thanks to years of psychic training with my Spirit Guides and Ascended Masters, I managed to escape safely but not unharmed. However, imagine just how much damage that type of attack would have on me if I weren't as prepared. A person without this type of experience nor training, would not so easily be able to withstand just the psychic sight of the Devil alone. And on the bright side, her attack was honestly the push I needed to write about it. As there are negative experiences there are always the positive equilibrium of the happening.

No one is immune to attacks by a black witch or wizard, but none are also unable to counter those attacks. Each person is competent and able to fight against these forces without harming those who cast the spell.

BLACK MAGICK TOOLS

The objects chosen by a Black magick wielder will depend on the individual's style and what they're trying to accomplish. Not all casters will use the same devices, nor will they use something always store-bought. Often the caster may choose to create their ritualistic devices in the privacy of their own home or wherever the person feels most comfortable during the ritual. Rituals are essential to the caster. It doesn't matter how it's conducted to public opinion, for the witch or wizard will use their intuitive skills and magick in harmony with their vibration to bring the best success to their spells—everything matters in a ritual. Where magick lies, so does the person's ability to harness all their focus and intention on the ritual conducted. Some rituals may take only a few minutes with little effort, whereas some may take a few hours to a few days to even weeks. Each level has its cause and effect and requirements on the caster.

Devices used in a spell cast by a White Witch or Warlock will harness the immense positive energy charged by the caster. Devices in magick depend on the person's personality and what ultimately works for them. There isn't necessarily a right or wrong way when casting a spell (as long as no harm is done to another or to oneself). All that truly matters is whether it helps the person to remain focused during the ritual and for it to aid in achieving their mystical goal through the power of focus and intention. Magick works best through the powers of the mind as all of one's energy is charged by emotions and thoughts. The more powerful the intention, the more powerful the spell will be.

Some of the devices used by a Black Caster will be charged by extreme forces of toxic and malevolent energy. This energy will bring harm to your aura and the whole body and soul energy. Excessive negative energy-charged, used, and cast by a black caster can trans mutate energy into a dark and murky sludge of toxic vibrations. These vibrations usually correlate to demonic power due to the caster working with demonic spirits or devil entities. The longer a caster works with the damned, the more damned their energy will be. Due to this, the devices won't be charged at all but subjected to an abusive energetic abomination. Baneful power cast by a Black magician through devices causes the devices themselves and any other items used during the ritual to become cursed. Automatically, they can be in conjunction with the curse cast to be also placed within the items used. In theory, the moment one touches an item used in a Black magick ritual will be cursed. This is true. This theory is not only correct but is fact-based on years of demonic research founded by paranormal investigators *Ed and Lorraine Warren*. Ed was a respectable Demonologist acknowledged by the catholic church who knew the ins and outs of demons and devils through a wide range of the occult. Lorraine was a highly skilled Clairvoyant who used her abilities to help identify the spirits haunting their clients and spotting dark magick. Each of their cases was meant to educate the public in better protection from hostile supernatural forces. The Warrens not only were able to identify the magickal intention, but the spirits summoned, devices used, spells and incantations conjured, and where and when it was taken place. Psychically, the Warrens were able to produce the evidence required to identify the cult or people involved and even kept the devices used to better protect others from further supernatural harm. The evidence from the Warrens towers over three thousand cases, and over one hundred cursed and haunted artifacts are carefully stored in their famous haunted museum in Connecticut today.

If the Warrens could identify these types of attacks and devices, so can you! They were not superhuman, but ordinary yet extraordinary people determined to help those haunted and tortured by Hell's malevolence. Without question, the types and number of devices used in a ritual would blow your mind. There are so many ways a caster can use something as mundane as a wristwatch, toys, jewelry to a harmless mirror and turn it into one of the most dangerous objects on the planet. Below is a list of some of the most common devices used during a Black magick ritual but are not limited to only the items mentioned below.

BLACK MAGICK TOOLS COMMONLY USED IN CURSES

- **Mundane objects connected to the victim** the caster uses for a curse or a hex.

- **Store-bought or homemade vodou doll** made to look like the victim. The doll will usually have hair from the victim, a piece of clothing, or even sprayed the same perfume the victim often wears. Vodou dolls are commonly used in Vodou or Hoodoo, depending on the caster's alignment within their religion or style of craft.

- **Black and Red candles.** Black candles often signify the intention of death, depression, and destruction. Red candles correlate with blood, pain, lust, and suffering for the victim.

- **Blood of the caster** from a bloodletting ritual.

- **Blood of the victim.** How the blood is taken from the victim is endless. A curse to make a woman infertile, for example, can include the menstrual blood of the victim. (How the caster was to get this blood is left to the imagination and horror of the reader).

- **A blood sacrifice** of an animal, a rodent, insects to human beings. (Need I say more?)

- **A dagger.** Daggers are used during Black magick rituals to cut, stab, or slice the vodou doll that represents the targeted victim. The blade may also be used to cut themselves during bloodletting or sacrifice an animal or person.

- **A mirror.** It's often believed that mirrors are a doorway to other realms. Mirrors are used in magick for many spells, including beauty or glamour magick. However, in Black magick, mirrors are often used to trap evil spirits to unleash the evil spirit against their victim when the mirror is gifted to their prey.

- **Spells written in blood or red ink** in a book, journal, on a piece of parchment, or on a wall.

- **Demonic and Devil Sigils.** Sigils are specific symbols used to summon and work with spirits. All spirits, good and evil, have their sigil, like their signature in the universe. Black Magick will often accompany a demonic or devil sigil written on the caster or tattooed. At times, the caster will write/ draw the sigils of the demons and devils they work with on the items and devices used during their rituals or somewhere on the land/ property.

- **Animal or human bones, including skulls.** This may seem appropriate to set the mood during Halloween, but these remains are not used for aesthetics. Though fresh flesh sacrificed is most desired to the demonic, remains of the dead are often used in Black magick as a subtle yet morbid replacement. If a caster wishes death upon their victim but doesn't want to make a traditional sacrifice, the use of animal or human remains will often be displayed on or within the altar. (Again, how the caster acquires these bones/remains is left to the reader's suspicion).

- **A picture or drawing of the victim.** A picture is often used for the caster to send the curse accurately and effectively to their desired target.

BLACK MAGICK ENCOUNTER

It's often believed in the spiritual and psychic community that psychic attacks caused by Black magick are sporadic -but I express certainly that's not only untrue but dangerously naïve. Although it may not be your typical engagement in your daily routine, that doesn't mean it's impossible. As there are good people on this planet with the best intentions, others walk with forces of darkness capable of the worst kind of apathy.

Encountering a location where Black magick has been done, one thing is for sure, **NEVER** touch the items used! If you happen to enter a room with evidence of Black magick by some unfortunate circumstance, it's sincerely recommended to leave the premises *immediately*. Unless you wish to have something like a demon sent to your home, or a terrible curse conjured with intentions to bring hell on earth to you and your family, it's better to leave everything where you found it. Never touch or take anything that was used in a Black magick ritual. Those who have taken items from dark rituals inevitably became cursed, were haunted by ferocious spirits, mysteriously disappeared forever, or were tragically found dead. To best prevent this scenario, the best thing to do is to leave calmly and respectfully, not to cause a scene. If you don't want to offend anyone, make up some harmless excuse for why you must depart. Though it would make sense, to be honest, sometimes it's wise to keep one's thoughts to themselves and leave while you still can. People in Black magick will curse those who dare say anything against their chosen gods, demons, and devils. As the saying goes, if you have nothing nice to say, then don't say anything at all. In a situation where you may feel psychically threatened, it would be wise.

If you ever encounter a Black magick caster, always keeping your psychic guard up is highly advised. Black magick wielders tend to lose sight of the difference between opinion from hate. I've met many who tend to become easily offended when stating spiritual truths or difference in opinion through love regardless of how respectable one is. It's crucial and inadvisable to test or dare those who work with evil. There's no level of evil Black magick doesn't cross. All energy used in Black magick is pure malice, intended for one thing -to bring chaos and damn all who it encounters.

Although it may be tempting to assume that every misfortunate happening is caused by a curse or a hex, it's imperative to remain logical. Not everything that is seemingly unfair is caused by Black Magick. Sometimes life will throw us a few curve balls that we aren't always able to deflect. Not everything that appears bad is due to a hex or a curse, so it's important to remain open to interpretation of all things through the lens of common sense and careful analysis.

After the attack by "Demon Kandy," I knew it was time to write this book. I always knew I would write a book that would help others against dark forces, but it was never on my to-do list, believe it or not. I was focused on enlightenment and demonology, but silly enough, the idea of psychic protection never seemed to be at the top. Now, when I think about it, I'm baffled by that too. After the attack, I knew it was time to get more serious on the matter. My intuition knew it was now or never.

No matter how much one attempts to ignore these universal threats, they will always be there. The good news is you have a choice. Either ignore it and pray it doesn't come after you or face it and overcome it. Fear isn't the motivation of this book, no matter how many times someone tries to spin it. No, sir, it is courage that is the motivation. Looking into what manifests evil with courage guides understanding its mystery and better protecting from its treachery.

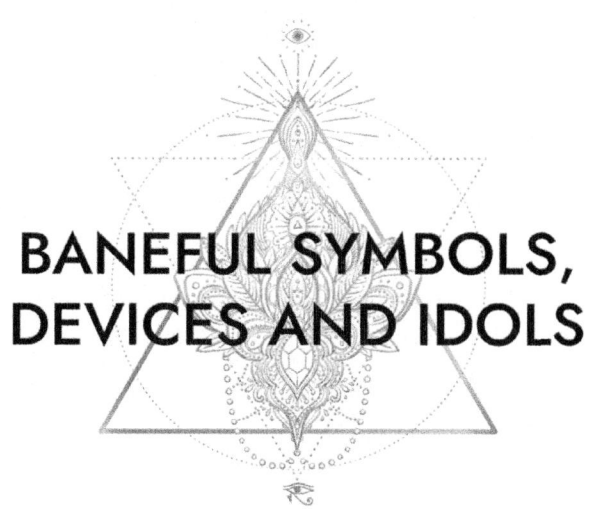

BANEFUL SYMBOLS, DEVICES AND IDOLS

CHAPTER FIVE

Demonic symbols can be found nearly everywhere. There are different forms of satanism in almost every aspect of life. Satanism and Demonic icons can be found in photos, clothing, movies, music, art, statues, and video games. The list is endless. Of course, this isn't said to instill panic but bring awareness of satanism's daily encounters that are nearly unavoidable. Satanic symbolism is found in the satanic temples and a wide range of demonic expressions. Demonolaters and Satanists have made it a part of their mission to spread primary evil across the nation, for the more followers, the better. The more ways Satanic elements and their artifacts can be sneaked into daily life, the easier it is to gain further power, influence, and control over humanity.

We've covered the dangers of Baneful Rituals and their followers; now it's time to go over some of the more popularized expressions of Demonic ideology. What is listed are not the only forms of Demonic symbolism and artifacts but are the more common ways it's manipulated and maneuvered into everyday usage. Satanic elements are placed within nearly everything. The more one is made aware of these symbols, artifacts, and idols, the greater your chances at defending and deflecting a future foe.

To best identify malevolence, the images provide guidance for further awareness. It wouldn't serve you well if these images, were not placed for reference.

- **Baphomet.** Satanic temples often have the malevolent horned goat god Baphomet erected. This god can create and commit the worst types of horrors imaginable. Those who follow, use, or are around this statue are haunted by nightmares past expectations. None are without warning when in the presence of this primary devil. Baphomet is one of the more popular deities idolized as a cornerstone of worship

and representation of the Satanic belief. To the Satanist, Baphomet isn't evil rather a symbolism of balance and equilibrium of both dark and light energy. Baphomet is very real and relies heavily on negative energy by enslaved people in Hell and those he tortures. Baphomet images are often placed within the entertainment industry: Satanic temples, clothing, statues, and even tattoos. This is the same devil spirit that many demonically influenced witches believe to be a benevolent representation of dualism of the universe and you. *They are sorely mistaken.*

- **Inverted Pentagram.** Witches and Wiccans find excellent protection and magickal aid with the traditional pentagram; typically, a five-pointed star pointed upright. However, it's  customary in Satanism to pervert what has been sought as refuge and guidance in magick and spiritualism. When the pentagram is in reverse and is positioned upside-down, it's now become the symbol for the demonic. Those who work with Black Magick will often wear clothing with this symbol, have tattoos, jewelry, art on their walls as a form of tribute, to a simple wallpaper on their cellphone. Inverted pentagrams are used in Black Magick rituals, curses, and frequently during Satanic ceremonies, depending on the individual.

- **666.** As silly as this may seem, it's highly advised to be wary of this number at all costs. Within Numerology, Angels' numbers  will often be linked in threes and patterns. Numbers like 111, 333, 777, 1818, 1212, and so on are taught to be high vibrational numbers given and presented by Heaven and its angels to guide us. In Numerology, the number 9 is associated with humanity and humanitarianism, whereas the number 6 is related to the material world, finances, and ego. It's easy to see that when you flip the number 9, it becomes a 6. The 9 no longer represents the moral code of humanity based on love, kindness, and goodness; instead, it becomes another inverted disconnection from what we humans call humane. Angels' numbers have been known throughout the ages but so have the devil's descended vibrations. It's a widespread debate the number 666 doesn't mean the devil; instead, is a reference to the material world and finances -however, I've come to find truth in this number through personal experience. Nearly every time I am attacked or approached by a demon or a devil spirit, I somehow catch sight of this number. At first, I denied its presence and would throw it off as a coincidence. However, the more frequent these attacks occurred, the more I took notice of the devil's number. Numbers hold energetic vibrations closely concerning what it symbolizes. As Angels and benevolent beings have positive vibrations, so does evil in numbers.

- **Demon Tarot.** Satanic symbolism has managed to nudge its way into traditional and ancient divination methods and tools. Tarot cards are not evil, nor are they meant nor designed to summon nor work with deities specifically. The conventional tarot like the Raider Waite deck, for example, was designed to aid those in divination through spiritual and intuitive guidance. Never was the deck intended to conjure the primary evil like devils and demons. Unfortunately, several companies have so carelessly created Demonic tarot and oracle decks much like the traditional tarot for the sake of wealth. Depending on design and booklet instruction, these decks cross between an oracle or tarot. Traditional tarot will have one card identified as the "Devil" to represent addiction, toxic relationships, and situations in a reading. This card can also describe the devil if someone were experiencing a demonic haunting, but typically, this is not always the case in a reading.

A Demon tarot deck, the cards will be a wide range of demonic spirits and devils depicted in grave detail. These decks though they state, are not meant to summon demons or devils -the booklets will suggest otherwise. As I'm a collector of tarot cards, I've discovered there to be some grave concern that will not only invite evil into your home but into your life entirely. Evil spirits have the power to influence those that we'd least expect, like affecting a full-blown company or a single designer to manifest these for the human population. It's not coincidental that these reached the market, as it's again the Satanist's dutiful promise to ensure there's a devil available at your door or, in this case, your tarot deck. If you were to encounter this type of deck, it's wise not to touch or use the items and leave them where you found them. Just utilizing a Demon tarot and occult decks will inadvertently invite the demonic spirits to your home, whether you intended it or not.

- **Inverted Cross.** Satanism's motivation is to destabilize what it counters, and in this case, it's Christianity. Though I'm not a Christian now, I was for years and intuitively knew the inverted cross is a direct insult to Yehoshua (Jesus Christ).  Jesus exists and has instructed with guidance during my years as a Psychic Medium that Satanism is closely linked with Hell. Traditionally Christianity's cross is pointed upright, representing the sacrifice of Jesus Christ and for the love of humanity. As usual, Satanism took the cross and flipped it upside down, meaning the exact opposite of what Christianity stands for. Satanism embodies the desires of the flesh without apologies which goes against all that the Christian faith upholds. Though I don't quite agree with Christianity or any type of dogma, the insult to Christianity by inverting the cross aligns demonic nature. Devils take what is honored in good faith and taint it without mercy. Therefore, if you encounter people wearing this inverted symbol, it's best to be guarded. The inverted cross is often displayed in posters and other art ranges, tattoos, music, clothing, jewelry, and statues. This symbol intends to demonstrate one's loyalty to the demonic, Satanic worship, Devil worship, and through Black Magick.

- **The Symbol of Lucifer.** Although this isn't a Satanic symbol, it's used and worshiped by Luciferins. Luciferins will wear this symbol in respect to their deity Lucifer as a form of worship and protection during  rituals, ceremonies, and in Black Magick. Luciferins believe Lucifer is viewed as a misunderstood deity innocently sharing enlightenment and knowledge of the universe. Lucifer's symbol inserted inside an apple gains attention to the average person through a basic understanding of the Bible in the association of Adam and Eve. The apple represents to Luciferins the forbidden fruit of knowledge bitten and consumed by those who seek truth through enlightenment. One of the many reasons why the phrase "enlightenment" has been given such a bad rep due to this manipulative narrative done by Lucifer himself. Enlightenment is neither good nor evil but is a state of new awareness given to the one that seeks another level of perception. However, there is nothing here but deception and manipulation. Lucifer is a Fallen Angel who works with demons and devils. Don't be so easily fooled. Lucifer may be knowledgeable in many areas, but he is also a charming liar that will put you in dangerous situations with the wrong company.

- **Ouija Boards/ Séance.** Ouija Board, also known as a spirit board, or talking board, has been a popular paranormal tool for centuries. A typical/  traditional Ouija Board is a flat board marked with the letters of the alphabet, with the numbers 0-9, the words "yes," "no," occasionally "hello," and "goodbye," along with various symbols and images. It comes with a planchette, a small heart-shaped piece of wood or plastic, designed to move as an indicator on the board to spell out messages during a séance. The participant(s) place their fingers on the planchette, moving about the board to spell out words or messages.

The game is so famous one can so easily acquire a Ouija board in your local store where toys are sold. A child as young as eight years old can purchase this item and take it home with full intention to connect with the spirit realm. As innocent as this game may seem, it's not a game at all. No amount of mental prep can properly prepare even a grown adult for what may come to pass from using this device. A traditional Ouija board enables telepathic communication between the participants and the other side. When the séance begins, this initiates the opening of a psychic portal. Due to this cosmic psychic energy, the entities present or those who hear the psychic call of invitation will use this portal to enter the earth realm. Unless the participants have a Guardian Angel with them or proper Spirit Guides (that still doesn't guarantee protection), this is a danger to all involved. Ouija Boards have attracted low vibrational spirits like Earth-Bound human souls that refuse to ascend past the earth realm. These spirits are often souls that take on the mortal realm as their own and manipulate humanity greedily. Earth-bound spirits are commonly murderers, rapists, thieves, narcissists, abusers, drug addicts, alcoholics, serial killers, etc. These souls remain on earth to continually take advantage of the living through exact situations like a séance. It's like a buffet of energy right for the picking that enables these spirits to attach to the participants for selfish desires easily. Ouija Boards don't attract just Earth-Bound human spirits; however, they immensely attract demons, devils, and other negative vibrational spirits. Demons are known for haunting Ouija Boards to gather more victims through the board.

When the Ouija Board séance is completed, and the participant uses the planchette to say "goodbye" -notably, this doesn't end the séance communication and especially doesn't close the psychic portal that has been opened. As uncomfortable as this may sound, this is factual. For once a psychic portal has been extended by something like a séance or through a Ouija Board séance; the only way it can be shut appropriately is by high vibrational spirits like Angels, Starseeds, and other deities like benevolent Gods and Goddesses. Though one's intentions may be to close communication, the unfortunate reality is this invitation has already granted the demonic or low vibrational spirits to take the reins of this communication. Most participants that enter a Ouija Board session do so without this in mind, nor with the proper psychic training to protect and defend against these types of supernatural threats. This is where it's necessary to abide by psychic awareness like this that just may save you from a nightmare you may never forget. Most Ouija Board sessions may appear innocent on the surface and even dull without anything happening. However, for a few days to even hours, those participants may notice an uncomfortable and unfamiliar presence in the home.

Ouija Boards aren't the only spirit boards; regrettably, more sinister boards are created. Demonic Ouija Boards have been spotted on eBay, Etsy, and other online stores by sellers who make the board with full intention to summon demonic spirits. Other sellers will share they've discovered these boards and want them out of their home immediately with a warning label attached. No good thoughts will attract positive experiences or positive spirits to a Ouija Board. It doesn't matter if one has good vibrations or intentions. As long as there remain low vibrational spirits on the earth realm, there'll remain low vibrational encounters and consequences through Ouija Boards.

- **Conduits (Demonic Attached Items).**
Conduits form an energetic attachment of a spirit to an item. Demonic entities and Devils often create conduits to manipulate the impression of possessing an item that is often considered haunted.
The Demons, Devils, and other evil spirits will target an item they view will greater the chances of human attachments and interactions. This enables the evil spirit to effortlessly become invited into the human's aura and life, enticing the demon to move through to the next haunting phase.

Spirits don't possess things -they possess people. When a person experiences paranormal activity in a home or a location, they don't say their house is possessed; they say it is haunted. This same rule applies to items. Items that become attached by demons don't mean we should imagine a giant grim monster clinging to a doll while sucking its thumb. As humorous of an image that is, it's far more dissatisfying. Demonic spirits will remain positioned next to or lay on the item while they patiently wait for their next unsuspecting victim. An item like a doll, for example, is a perfect conduit for a demon seeking to possess a child. Demons and other low vibrational spirits have no concept of time; thus, a few hundred years doesn't affect their patience. Demons have been reported to attach to chairs, desks, jewelry, mirrors, statues, dolls, toys, land, houses, buildings, etc. Items that become conduits are now the demon's property. Anyone who touches, defiles, disturbs, or insults that property or entity often mistakenly regret it.

- **Dybbuk Box.** A Dybbuk box or Dibbuk box is a wine cabinet, or other kinds of chests claimed to be haunted by a  dybbuk spirit. In Jewish mythology, a dybbuk is a possessing evil spirit believed to be the dislocated soul of a dead person. It supposedly leaves the host body once it has successfully fulfilled its goal, sometimes after being exorcised.

A Dybbuk Box is connected with Jewish folklore where a dark spirit is said to take over the bodies of living people and uses them for evil. Legend has it, a Dybbuk is trapped inside the box to prevent harm to the living. Once the box has been opened or tampered with in any way, the evil spirit will violently haunt and attack the living.

Zak Bagans the host and lead Paranormal Investigator of *Ghost Adventures* has purchased a Dybbuk from a man named Jason Haxton and placed it on display at The Haunted Museum that he owns and runs. Zak has highly reported, and those who have been around the Dybbuk to have undergone severe paranormal terror. Experiences like seeing dark shadow figures, hearing growls, unexplained sounds, lights flickering, objects moving to glass smashing without scientific explanation. In addition, there have been reports of Zak's Museum visitors leaving with horror stories of their own. Security cameras displayed throughout the museum have caught glimpses of dark transparent figures moving around the location to spot the visitor's unexpected preternatural attacks, leaving them to flee the museum in fear for their lives.

Dybbuk Boxes became a horror trend by influencers, paranormal investigators, and those searching for a twisted adrenaline rush. There are disturbing YouTube videos of influencers teaching how to create a Dybbuk. The more Dybbuk boxes are made, the more hell can break loose on earth. As every religion has its version of good, so are its expressions of evil. It's not a toy. It's through my understanding from my Spirit Guides that Dybbuk boxes work like a genie in a bottle, only instead of getting three wishes, you get cursed. Dybbuk spirits are known to curse those who mess with them in any way, thus have learned to put people in danger to even an early grave. My advice would be to avoid a Dybbuk box at all costs! If you find yourself ever in the presence of one, remain respectful and withhold from insulting the Dybbuk in any fashion. Making fun of a Dybbuk spirit is no laughing matter.

- **Satanic Hand Sign.** Those who follow Satan, Demons, Devils, and spiritually involved with the demonic realm use this hand gesture to display their faith. The more common hand sign in resonance with Satan  worship is displayed. The hand sign can be done with the left or right hand, as long as the thumb presses down the two middle fingers. Often this hand sign is commonly mistaken with the rock-and-roll sign. However, the pinky finger and the index finger represent the devil's horns. Devil worshippers and Satanists use this sign to honor their descended god of choice or the demons they work with. Satanists that use this sign in public or in photographs do so with full awareness and intention of the controversy. Though a Satanist's courage and honor are admirable, the sign usage brings awareness to negative spirits like demons to attract more towards them like a psychic call even if the Satanist and Devil worshipper aren't aware. Those that use this hand sign will often do so unapologetically. My professional advice is to respect their chosen faith and remain fully aware of their intentions. Not all Satanists, Devil worshippers, or Demonolaters are well-intended individuals. Many are good people with the best intentions; however, several within this community take it to extreme measures beyond the realm of darkness.

- **Curses and Cursed Items.** Curses have been around for centuries, as far back as the ancient Egyptian and Mayan era. Items that become cursed will have a different outcome depending on the intention of the curse by the  dark caster. No affliction is subject to the same result, nor are they conducted in the same fashion. Often curses are crafted with malevolent spirits that aid the magician in their evil plan. A cursed item will harness immense harmful energy isolated to the item but will affect anyone and anything it touches or is around. Evil powers by malicious spirits will intercept the object, creating a toxic link/attachment to the item. Once the curse has been complete, the item is forever cursed until the curse has been lifted. Curses on objects and people range from limitless intentions and grim probabilities. Most curses are crafted to cause significant pain and hardship to the victim(s). It can vary from minor bad luck to wishing severe suffering and even death to several people at once. There is a broad debate on curses within the occult community. Many are under the belief curses cannot be broken when they're set in motion, but I've discovered this is entirely false! Curses absolutely can be reversed and prevented before it manifests. Just because the ritual is completed doesn't mean the manifestation of that curse is irreversible. One must not lose hope, as there are evil beings; benevolent beings are fully capable of reversing and stopping a curse in its tracks!

Lifting curses is tricky, and not all Psychics, Demonologists, and occultists may know how to lift a curse or a hex. Therefore, if you feel you've been affected by a curse, it must be evaluated by well-experienced spiritualists with a mysticism background in the occult, magick, and Demonology.

- **Paranormal and Occult Apps.** Our modern age has drastically adapted to nearly everything becoming digitalized, including the supernatural. Today you can find hundreds of phone apps designed to contact the spirit realm that uses electromagnetic waves and other  methods. Some of the apps are free, whereas others require a fee. The risks of using these apps are incredibly high. When a person begins to use the app to allow a psychic call out into the universe just like a séance, it then emits permission to any low vibrational spirit to make contact. Though you may not intentionally create a portal and psychic call while participating with a circle of friends, the app does this for you in a matter of seconds. Do apps create psychic portals?

-Not necessarily, but not impossible! A portal can develop depending on the person using the app and how psychically evolved and determined they are in establishing contact. How often the person was to use these apps also significantly matters. These apps can be increasingly addictive and can cause a psychic attachment to the entities contacting the person using this app on their phone or device. This can create a conduit by a harmful extension from a malicious spirit to your device without being the wiser.

The other metaphysical risk is the occult apps specifically designed and dedicated to demons and devils. For example, Black Magick occultists have established impressive apps crafted with the innate intention to conjure and contact demons and devils. These apps range from working with demons, spells, curses to open possession methods.

Those who wish to use these apps obviously will use them at their own risk. It's not advised, nor is it recommended in my opinion, but if one were to do so, you do so with the full awareness of the possible, said consequences.

- **Demonic Imagery.** Although this may be common sense, it's prevalent to mention. Not always will demonic influences be so obvious. Sometimes it takes a trained eye to spot sinister  suggestiveness, especially art. A devilish t-shirt, for example, may have an assortment of bones, blood, violence, and gore. And though it may not have satanic symbols doesn't mean the imagery may not possess the symbolism. Artistic expression is viral in Satanism and Demonolatry. Other controversial images may be bestiality or a woman mounting a devilish goat figure. Sexual stimulation and disturbing imagery flatter Satanists' imagination and enrich the devil's grasp on its followers. Pornography with demons and devils like Succubus (sexual female demon) and Incubus (sexual male demon) is overtly famous. Demonic porn in anime or manga is regrettably one of the more common expressions grown in dark fantasy. Do not be fooled into believing that just because it's a television show or a film that it wasn't created by the forces of evil. Devils have a vast engagement and powerful influence in the media, entertainment industries, and extensive levels of modern-day activities.

- **Satanic Child Grooming.** Don't think for a minute the Satanic Temples, churches, and cults are not interested in grooming your child. Satanic clubs for children have been slowly rising as they use the religious freedom narrative. In early 2022, a Satanic Temple was pushed at a public school by opening and operating a Satanic Club for children.  The option is free for anyone willing; however, it's been led to my attention they plan to make this a national opportunity for all. As no one should be denied their religious freedom, it doesn't include the right to groom a child towards eternal damnation. Children are the easier prey within any type of cult or influence. Children are a prime target in the devil's eyes, for it enables them free range of energetic and emotional effects without the child ever knowing. A child is easily susceptible to suggestion and influence, creating the perfect buffet for demonic entities. Demons and Devils make it their mission to harness enough sheep to feed and gather souls to take to Hell. What better way than to use the parent's already altered state of awareness and inject the child's open mind with contaminated immorally inaccurate information.

It's highly advisable to remain aware of your child's school activities or other public/ private functions. Secretly Devils crave the innocence of a child the most as they're incapable of defending themselves from harm or negative attachments.

- **The Leviathan Cross.** The sign of Leviathan is sometimes referred to as the cross of Satan, which means "Satan's Cross." The double cross symbolizes protection and balance between persons.  The infinity symbol at the bottom underlines the infinite nature and commonly represents the eternal universe. This is the ideology in the church of Satan and what the followers believe. However, Leviathan is also a devil spirit capable of the worse kind of affliction. Therefore, one will often catch sight of this cross as a tattoo, on jewelry, posters, and other levels of outward expression.

- **Pizzagate.** As many of us can sit and enjoy a hot pizza with all of our favorite toppings without a second thought, this is one of the more uncommon and more sinister symbols in Satanism. Simply  consuming pizza is not Satanic -breathe, you can still enjoy pizza! However, in 2016 a disturbing conspiracy theory that went viral during the United States presidential election circulated. It has been extensively investigated and discredited by various organizations, including the Washington, D.C. police. It was believed that people in power within the government were heavily involved in child sex rings through the code of ordering a pizza. Each topping would supposedly represent the age, ethnicity, gender, type of sexual activity, and how many children.

Although this was discredited, it hasn't stopped Satanists from using this for disturbing amusement. Frequently Satanic coloring books will have a demonic-faced pizza doing suggestive violence while holding a knife dripping with pizza sauce. Often missed by parents, you may spot a child wearing a pizza shirt. A simple image of a pizza is nothing to worry over; however, a pizza with demonic symbolism or any kind of violence is relative to the wicked. As the conspiracy spread, so has the Satanic symbolism. Something as innocent as pizza is now part of the demonic code in the voice of Satan. Be aware of any images with a piece of pizza, for it just may be a slice of the devil.

- **Demonic Influencers.** Typically social media wouldn't be of significant concern as it's not manufactured with the sole intention to solicit demons or satanism. However, there's been a widespread demonic trend hitting  social media accounts like TikTok, Instagram, Twitter, Facebook, YouTube, and many others. I began receiving loads of reaction requests from my fans informing me of people promoting Demonolatry and Satanism. TikTokers and other influencers on other social media apps share why they worship or work with demons and why it's "okay" and "safe" to do so. These "influencers" became famous simply by showcasing their left-hand path. For example, there are "psychics" on TikTok that state devils don't want your soul because they "can't do anything with it." Tiktok, for example, having over 1 billion users, it's not so safe to say there are millions of possible demon workers and worshippers trending what appears to be a potential second satanic panic. It's not a conspiracy but a brutal reality.

The music industry has equally been known to openly express its demonic agenda through several artists, and it's gotten worse. For example, Canadian singer *Celine Dion* partnered with a "gender-neutral" children's clothing line *Nununu* called *Celinununu*, in 2018. The clothing line exhibits children and adult models in Satanic attire with skulls, inverted stars, and crosses. On Nununu's Instagram page, images display several children posing with the

Satanic hand sign. If this wasn't disturbing enough, the word "Nu" translated in French is naked. For a children's clothing line, it's rather odd the creators would choose such a phrase that seems grossly inappropriate. In addition, Nununu's website address is titled Nununuworld.com, while some of the clothing clearly states "new world" -which again coincides with several conspiracy theories that are eerily accurately close.

Additionally, there have been claims allegding it's Pizzagate coming out and claiming their position of power and influence on children and adults alike. And though it wasn't received well by the general public aside from the ridiculously high prices, some major celebrities have been spotted with their children wearing the line. Celinununu clearly states they want to use their clothing line to mold children's thinking to create and adapt to a genderless world. Some would say this is an effort to brainwash the already naïve minds of the young, not even to know themselves upon birth. Lastly, the logo name Nununu as designed in the picture below, is close to displayed on their website.

nununu

If you were to take an inverted copy of this name and place it directly under the upright version, you would see this in the second image. It would display what appears to be a mirror image of the name Nununu.

ΟΧΟΧΟΧ

But then, if you take the name Nununu a third time and place an upright Nununu overlapping the bottom half atop of the previous two, you would discover the number 666 in the third attempt! Hard to identify at first, but the following image reveals the hidden message.

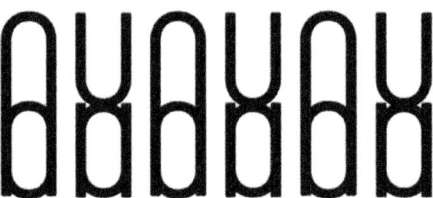

Call me a conspiracy theorist all you want, but that speaks louder to me than usual. Something about that name just didn't sit right with me, and when I played around with the title, I discovered this within a matter of seconds. Nununu should've been called **Nonono!**

If that isn't distubring enough, in 2021, *Lil Nas X* released a song and music video on YouTube titled Montero *(Call Me By Your Name)*. The rapper's controversy went viral, soaring over 444 million views in less than one year. Lil Nas X's song was a personal expression as a gay man judged by Christians. It could've been relatable; however, he decided to jump into the pit of hell and began grinding on a devil as a fallen angel in the music video. Soon after, Lil Nas X released a Satan shoe line of black and red shoes that contained actual human blood within every shoe. Unfortunately, Lil Nas X isn't the only rapper who's chosen the dark side. The Australian rapper *Iggy Azalea* came out with a perfume commercial in 2022 titled *Devil's Advocate,* while too getting down and dirty with a she-devil or what appeared to be a succubus. I'm a fan of Iggy, but even this was disturbing.

This does not suggest that the social media apps and people mentioned or others like them are evil intended, devout Satanists, or considered dangerous. However, this highlights that the chances of encountering someone who walks with demons, or are so easily manipulated by the demonic are a greater risk than ever anticipated. Who one follows or idolizes in the like is one's personal decision but tread with caution. Social media and influencers may be the hit trend now, but eventually, the darker they are, the harder they fall.

Where an individual resides within their heart is where they shall lead. Human souls are meant to expand and transcend into a better version of themselves, and it's through positive and negative experiences where growth happens. However, not all those who walk among us have benevolent intentions. The symbols, devices and idols mentioned are not the only threats but are the most likely to be encountered in daily life. It's been said that bringing awareness of these supernatural threats promotes negative thinking thus attracts the unwanted. However, I've come to develop a sense of respect through the gift of simple understanding. The more one is aware, is most likely to know when, where, and how to find the exit, from possible future harm.

BANEFUL THREATS

CHAPTER SIX

It's never easy accepting one's vulnerability, nor the fact some people will take advantage of that vulnerability. And unfortunately, it doesn't stop there. There's another level of hostility ready and armed to take on your entire aura and sense of livelihood. This type of threat goes beyond the physical senses yet can indefinitely harm the human body, mind, and spirit. However, you will be relieved to know that the following don't happen often, but that doesn't mean they are rare or impossible.

PSYCHIC ATTACK

Hopefully, you may never experience these forms of attacks, but it doesn't mean we shouldn't cover the dangers and their possibilities. There's a powerful surge of vibration within everyone and everything that can be used for good or evil. This central source of energy that connects us all in unison can have a positive or a negative effect. Depending on one's emotions and the thoughts charged by those emotions, one can develop beneficial or harmful outcomes for others. The energy guided by the deepest desires and intentions through the will of one's thoughts will trigger the powers of one's psychic abilities. Whether one is aware of this happening, the energy has no choice but to listen and manifest those mental and emotional desires.

For example, when a person sends a loved one good wishes, let's say to get well, for good luck, or simply love, this sends a positive charge toward the person they're sending those thoughts. The intentional order of energy becomes a force that travels to the other person to provide support through loving energy. This benevolent power can aid the other person to experience good feelings like confidence, healing, security, love, and hope. However, not all people send good intentions; instead wish nothing but the worst to those they despise. Vice versa, when a person sums up enough hate, anger, jealousy, and hostility toward another, that energy, whether intentional or not, will have a sizable negative impact on the other person. Energy has a remarkable way of acting on what one thinks with just enough intention and focus.

WHAT IS A PSYCHIC ATTACK?

To describe it plainly, a ***psychic attack*** *is either intentional or unintentional negative psychic energy that is targeted and sent* *toward an unsuspecting victim.* A psychic attack can be created through emotions, thoughtful intentions, and even magick. There is no limit to how psychic attacks can manifest from the source of the person responsible. Whether the person is a Psychic Medium, Witch, Warlock, Demonolater, Satanist, or an ordinary yet gifted person, the psychic attack sent can cause considerable harm to another.

The person sending the psychic attack frequently may not be aware they are doing it, but it can be as powerful. A person does not have to be mindful of their psychic abilities to send a psychic attack -and you'd be glad they didn't. In contrast, a person trained in knowing how to harness their psychic powers will possess a more significant risk and threat. The more prepared a person is in their psychic abilities and magick, the higher the damage potential through a psychic attack.

WHO CAN SEND A PSYCHIC ATTACK

As we are all energy, anyone can send and receive a psychic attack. Therefore, one does not need to be exceptionally psychically skilled in supernatural abilities to send an attack. However, living people are not the only beings capable of sending a psychic attack.

Spirits/ Ghosts and entities from other realms that are earth-bound have the capability of sending a living person a psychic attack. For example, a spirit can send numerous living forms of psychic attacks during a haunting. I'm afraid these attacks are not as rare as most psychics and authors will state or publish. As I hate to be the bearer of bad news, plenty of psychic attacks is sent to the living by spirits. Living people are not the only beings in existence capable and fully conscious of sending mystical threats. It's an unfortunate reality but a real one that must be stomached if one is willing to move forward bravely within the unseen realm. We are in a universe beyond just the Law of Attraction. Beyond the material world is a world among infinite levels of domains with spirits one could grossly imagine.

The energy that is sent received and harvested long and powerful enough can maintain that same velocity for years. Therefore, toxic residual energy on land can create countless forms of psychic attacks on the living. As discussed, prior, negative residual energy can commit terrible damage to the person's wellbeing, but one may be wondering how this works. This is due to the land becoming like a vessel of toxic energy that begins to grow and expand and take or hurt anything it touches. Psychically, when witnessing just how volatile negative residual energy is, one would more than likely describe the sight like an energy warzone. Without the proper psychic protection, negative residual energy can harm the living, animals, plant life, and nearly everything it contacts.

IDENTIFY A PSYCHIC ATTACK

One may be wondering, *"How can I tell when I'm under a Psychic Attack?"* -A psychic attack can affect the living person in countless ways. There is no limit an actual psychic attack cannot reach when delivered by even the most unskilled of persons. With just enough hateful energy with the purest intentions to harm another, the attack can do mild affliction to the most extreme damage. In some instances, identifying a psychic attack can be evident, whereas in others may be challenging. Identifying when one is under psychic attack can take years of practice in one's psychic abilities and properly noticing changes in one's energy frequency. Not always will a psychic attack be simple to spot, but with the following clues and tips I've provided, it may be sure to assist in sensing a possible attack.

If one suspects a possible psychic attack, it's safe to take time to analyze everything about you internally carefully. The mind can play tricks on us, so it's necessary to analyze the information presented and critic what you've discovered. It's also advisable to seek medical assistance from a licensed clinical physician if you cannot find the root of the cause of your suspected psychic attack. Ways to tell if you're under a psychic attack are to pay close attention to your body, mind, and emotions. You know your body better than anyone, and it's only loving to ensure your temporary temple is always safe. Though not all psychic attacks are apparent, it's essential to start with the basic observation of oneself. The list provided is set in a question format as a beginner's guide or a gentle reminder for those who are more experienced.

PSYCHIC ATTACK SIDE EFFECTS

- Do you feel as if you are not yourself? As if someone has taken over your emotions and thoughts?

- Do you feel excessively drained of energy suddenly or often without a medical cause of explanation?

- Do you tend to experience unpleasant thoughts uncontrollably?

- Do you have moments of sudden rage, sadness, depression, fear, or anxiety without a cause?

- When taking time to notice your own body and energy, does it feel heavy or abnormally unpleasant? Does the energy feel icky or unclean?

- Do you experience sudden headaches or body pains often without a medical explanation?

- Do you sense a large amount of energy? If so, does this energy feel like an uncomfortable charge like pins and needles?

- Do you feel pressure on your body when laying down or walking around? Does this pressure feel like something is attached to you or sitting on top of your head or stomach? -If so, is this uncomfortable and unexplainable?

If you've answered yes to several of these then it's possible you've been experiencing a supernatural affliction.

SIGNS OF A PSYCHIC ATTACK

After carefully questioning your mind and body, it's time to investigate the psychic phenomena often associated with psychic attacks. Depending on the one who sent the psychic attack, the signs can range from mild to the most severe. Each psychic attack has its own goal and plan thus can typically be identified through several psychic experiences and paranormal occurrences.

Although there are countless types of psychic attacks and how they can be sent, the list below is grounded in the most common of signs. These signs are only a select few and are not the only signs when attempting to identify a psychic attack correctly.

- Severe bad luck

- Nightmares of evil creatures

- Nightmares of being murdered or committing murder.

- Nightmares of people you know or know personally, and they attack you in the dream(s).

- Sudden impacts to the head or other parts of your body. This will feel like an intentional jab, stab, or slam to the body unexplainably.

- Painful pressure to the third eye. This will often happen when laying down to sleep or when meditating.

- Paranormal activity in the home or wherever you go that's negative.

- Feeling and or sensing a negative presence in the home or alone at night after awakening from a nightmare.

- Feel intense negative energy (vibes) in the home or within your aura.

- Experiencing an Astral Kidnapping or Astral Attacks when asleep or when physically awake by a person you know or by something frightening that cannot be typically identified.

- Experiencing sudden extreme depletion in health without a medical explanation or cause.

- Experiencing **Sleep Paralysis**. This is when an evil spirit paralyzes the unsuspecting victim during sleep state and sets upon the person various types of psychic attacks. The person will feel consciously awake, but the body is stiff, causing the person unable to move as they see, hear, and feel the spirit and the attack.

THE AURA

The way a person lives through behaviors and choices can affect the **Aura** that is not only guidance of one's emotions and blockages but as a protective shield. The aura is a barrier of energy that makes up the person's prime energy source. This aurific field consists of different levels of **Chakras** that enable the human body to function within the emotional and mental database that aids in sensing energies and energetic shifts. Psychically, the *aura is the soul's primary energy source of protection, guidance, and power.*

The aura allows the human body to know when it is healthy or unhealthy. Although the human body is a respectable machine with intrinsic healing properties and capabilities, it is thanks to the aura that informs the human psyche to be made aware of those bodily changes. When the body becomes ill, the aura receives immediate signals of those physical threats. Once the aura receives this psychic signal, the human's consciousness and intuition will begin to receive those messages through feelings and specific mental images that something changed. Because of the aura, the human body is capable of many things, being alive for one. Without the aura, the soul would not be capable of being stable and fully aware of one's inner self. The aura is immensely sensitive to everything it connects to, including other people's auras. Everything on the earth plane has its form of an energy source like the human aura, but the human aura is the most complex. Animals and plant life, too, have their aura. Without the aurific fields, connecting with the planet, animals, and other humans would be highly challenging. I envision and describe the aura like the human soul's own personal galaxy.

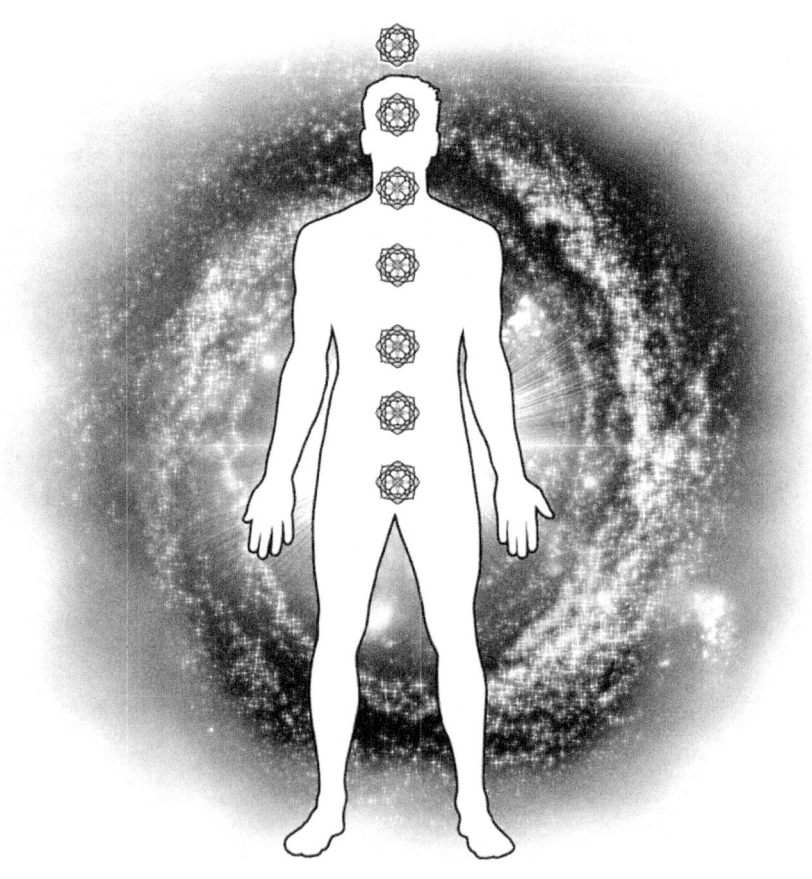

Every chakra plays a significant role for the human to remain grounded and the aura to remain balanced. How the person is affected positively or negatively through energy impacts the chakras. Emotions play an essential part in aiding the chakras to harmonize. If one of the chakras were to go out of balance, it would affect the entire aurific field. Like the human body, if one-part stops working, it can negatively impact the rest of the body. For example, if one were to get a cold or the flu and gets a stuffy nose, losing their sense of smell or breathing using the nose will also affect one's ability to taste food. The senses of the body all work together in harmony, but if even one goes out of whack, the rest of the parts either stop working or are too affected.

Seven main chakras affect the aura. Together we will cover the primary roles and discuss their importance and adverse effects on the mind, emotions, and body.

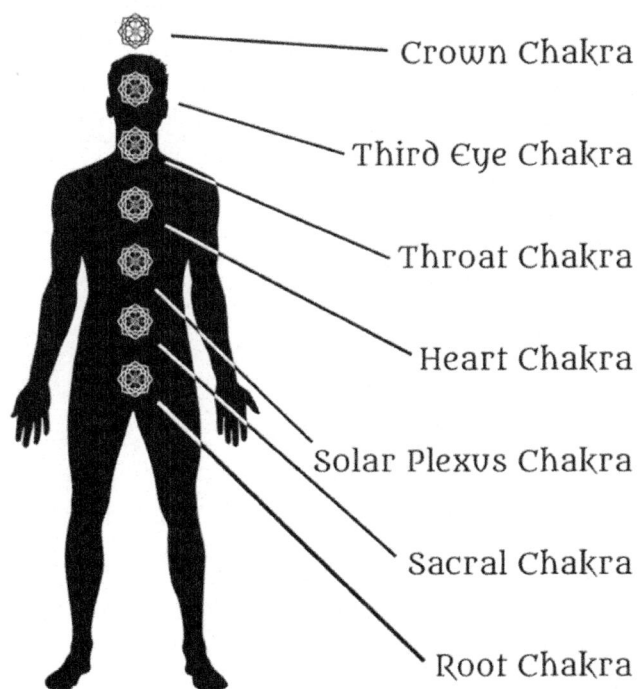

1. **CROWN CHAKRA:**
The crown chakra is one of the most important, yet it is one of the more difficult to harness for the majority population. This chakra enables intuition and divine guidance to be received and heard from Spirit Guides, Angels, Gods, Goddesses, Starseeds, and other benevolent beings. Opening and listening to one's Higher Self through the crown guides towards ascension and eternal transcendence. The primary purpose of the crown chakra is driven towards a higher state of consciousness and to receive messages from the universe.

CROWN CHAKRA ADVERSE EFFECTS:
Low vibrational energy and influences can close the crown chakra or keep it closed. For example, toxic relationships, influences, and cults involving brainwashing or grooming one away from independent thinking prevent the crown chakra from functioning and or opening. This can prevent a person from making clear decisions independently and wisely.

2. **THIRD EYE CHAKRA:**
The Third Eye Chakra enables one's higher perception and "sight" beyond this realm. The phrase "Opening one's Third Eye" stems from this chakra. When this second chakra has adequately opened, it grants universal and clear seeing of entities (spirits) and receives psychic visions. The Third Eye Chakra is the primary use for

Psychics, Mediums, Shamans, Witches, and those in a spiritual field or path.

THIRD EYE CHAKRA ADVERSE EFFECTS:
Negative low vibrational spirits, situations, lifestyles, and behaviors can significantly impact this chakra. Nearly anything negative can potentially close or prevent this chakra from opening or functioning. Therefore, when one wants their Third Eye Chakra opened, one must be willing to abandon unhealthy lifestyle choices to navigate better and harness this psychic connection. One cannot see until one is ready to cleanse one's eye of negativity.

3. THROAT CHAKRA:
The Throat Chakra is the third chakra that allows the person to speak one's truth clearly and confidently through communication. This chakra enables vocal freedom from oppression by talking openly. A healthy, balanced Throat Chakra shares deep feelings to purge unsettling emotional wounds. This chakra allows the person to keep secrets and keep their word faithfully, maintaining trust with others lovingly.

THROAT CHAKRA ADVERSE EFFECTS:
A blocked Throat Chakra prevents one from speaking lovingly and kindly. When negative energy impacts this third chakra, the individual will struggle to keep secrets, make promises, and tell their truth. Speaking unkindly with

excessive rudeness or sarcasm is another sign of a blocked Throat Chakra.

4. HEART CHAKRA:

This fourth chakra allows us to feel and connect deep within ourselves and others freely. A healthy Heart Chakra cares deeply about others' wellbeing and for themselves without fear of judgment. With a solid and loving heart, bonds develop fearlessly and tirelessly. An opened Heart Chakra enables a strong connection with the source of love, the universe, and with celestial beings.

HEART CHAKRA ADVERSE EFFECTS:

A blocked or unhealed heart can disproportionately impact self-love and accepting love from others. For example, when a Heart Chakra is unhealed from past pains and refuses to accept painful truths, this blocks the heart from loving oneself—creating a heavy heart, unable and unwilling to be loved or receive love. Likewise, toxic relationships that are abusive verbally, emotionally, sexually, and physically can weigh heavy on the heart chakra, causing it to close in reaction to self-protect. However, when the Heart Chakra closes, this turns into self-neglect of receiving love that prevents healing.

5. **SOLAR PLEXUS CHAKRA:**
   The fifth chakra is the Solar Plexus Chakra. This chakra is associated with confidence, self-esteem, self-worth, and listening to one's wellbeing and needs. In addition, this chakra allows one to stand up for themselves with conviction and truth with courage.

   SOLAR PLEXUS CHAKRA ADVERSE EFFECTS:
   A negative impact on the Solar Plexus Chakra will prevent and block one's ability to find confidence and believe in their self-worth. The blockage discourages one from finding courage and speaking in what they believe in with strength. Being in a negative or hostile work environment or being in a relationship where someone is demeaning, this block can negatively affect the Solar Plexus Chakra.

6. **SACRAL CHAKRA:**
   The Sacral Chakra is considered the center of the divine feminine and divine masculine energy. This is where sexuality and sensuality find a connection with self and others. This sixth chakra is also the center for creativity and emotional balance.

   SACRAL CHAKRA ADVERSE EFFECTS:
   When this chakra is blocked from negative energy or emotions, it prevents the person from expressing themselves sexually. The importance of this chakra is for the person to center their boundaries. Often what blocks

the Sacral Chakra is past or current sexual abuse left unhealed. When this chakra is blocked, a person may be unable to establish sexual boundaries or tend to give in to sexual invitations that aren't necessarily desired. Sexual intimacy will not be as pleasurable, and one may experience pain during intercourse. A blocked Sacral Chakra may affect the body, causing urinary tract infections or issues with ovaries for women. Men may experience a lack of sexual stimulation, be unable to perform sexually or urinary tract infections, etc.

7. **ROOT CHAKRA:**
The functions of the final Root Chakra are basic survival needs like food, shelter, and hygiene. Safety and security are also closely linked with this chakra, associated with protecting and providing for family and self. Finally, the utmost importance of this chakra is grounding and building/ maintaining a healthy foundation of one's livelihood.

ROOT CHAKRA ADVERSE EFFECTS:
Adverse effects of a Root Chakra include one unable to find balance or are unable or unwilling to make mature decisions. Reluctant to plan in creating a stable and secure lifestyle for self or one's family. Addiction, toxic relationships, and negative influences can block this chakra which backfires one's ability to become independent or financially stable.

THE AURA VULNERABILITY

Learning how to balance one's chakras and protecting the aura is psychically crucial for everything the human connects with has a positive or a negative effect on one's aurific field. Without the proper protection and balance, it can create severe issues for both the aura and the human body. As stated, the aura is a sensitive energy field. If the aura were to be compromised with unfamiliar sources like being exposed to Low vibrational energies, it could become weak. When an aura becomes weakened from overexposure to low vibrational energy or, to say, toxic energies, the person can be easily influenced and affected.

For example, when you're around a negative person, does it often leave you feeling drained, angry, or mentally exhausted? This is due to the other person's negative aurific field affecting your aura. On the other hand, a person with an aura that is balanced and positive, simply being around this person can be loving and healing, leaving you feeling upbeat and full of energy.

Auras positively charged and balanced will appear brightly colorful and harmonious with other auras. However, a negative aurific field can seem like a dark cloud or slimy black or grey-toned sludge. As the person thinks in one's thoughts with emotional guidance, it will navigate the aura to reciprocate those emotions and thoughts. One's aura has no choice, much like the Law of Attraction to shape and manifest into the mental waves of the human mind.

As mentioned earlier, thoughts are not the only thing that affects the aura; however, it's also with one's behaviors and choices. Low vibrational habits like drugs, alcohol, or abusive behaviors, for example, the aura will weaken significantly. Several things can negatively affect the aura, and it's essential to study this list in the following to use as a guide.

WHAT WEAKENS THE AURA

- Illegal drugs or drug addiction.

- Alcohol or alcohol addiction.

- Marijuana or marijuana addiction.

- Being involved in a gang or an aggressive group or cult.

- Demonolatry, Satanism, Luciferianism, or Satan/ Devil/ Demon worship.

- Necromancy, or any kind of Black Magick.

- Toxic relationships involving frequent hostility, physical and emotional abuse.

- Gambling or gambling addiction.

- Shopping addiction.

- Sex addiction like watching porn/ performing, excessive sexual entertainment as a stripper, dancer, etc.

- Hoarding items, food, etc.

- Anorexia or Bulimia and other eating disorders.

- Unhealthy eating, i.e., eating excessive amounts of junk food, sugary foods, fast food, etc.

- An unhealthy living lifestyle, i.e., not bathing frequently, lousy hygiene, an unclean home.

- Involved in crimes or other levels of deceptive behaviors and habits.

- Often in trouble with the law and refusing to abide by the law.

- Involved in indecent and immoral behaviors like abuse, crime, molestation, thievery, rape, etc.

RARE AND SEVERE PSYCHIC ATTACKS

In rare cases, perilous and hostile forces can send psychic attacks. These attacks are sporadic and are not typically experienced, even those in the spiritual/ psychic path. These types of severe cases of psychic attacks are sent by Demons, Devils, and those in Black Magick. It's not usually someone who will experience these forms of supernatural afflictions. Demonic entities and Devils have an insatiable desire to be entertained by torturing and haunting the living. Whenever one is to experience a psychic attack from primary evil, they will describe it as immensely painful and terrifying. Psychic Attacks by these powerful foes range from **Astral Kidnappings**, where they torture the living to get them to give in to the entity to take their soul. *Astral Kidnappings happen when a person is astrally pulled from their physical body by force unwillingly and taken to another dimension to be tortured or haunted.* People who experience this often may not realize it was a cosmic kidnapping and declare it a simple nightmare. However, nightmares don't pull your astral body out by force. Whenever someone is astrally attacked, their physical body will begin to show evidence of the affliction with bruises, scars, burns, cuts, etc. In rare scenarios, other forms of severe psychic attacks by primary evil can even lead to a fatal end to the living.

This isn't to suggest one is at fault when they experience a psychic attack. On the contrary. Though we can protect ourselves, that doesn't guarantee safety, nor does it prevent future psychic attacks. Where psychic attacks are involved, it's fair to suggest the evidence of spiritual warfare -that's what a psychic attack is. Psychic attacks are exactly what they are called "Psychic." In the realm of magick and the metaphysical, psychic attacks happen to the living on earth and other spirits on the other side (afterlife). Angelic beings of some of the greatest warriors like *Archangel Michael, Archangel Gabriel, the Egyptian God Horus* even the

Hindu God Lord Shiva have been through many psychic attacks. It doesn't matter if one is of the more ascended beings in the universe. As long as there's evil, there'll remain attacks from those who wish to commit harm. Thankfully, there are ways to protect from these malevolent types of energies and forces. In the following chapter, we will discuss the benefits of benevolence and how to defend against negative energies by enhancing and enriching your aura.

PART THREE:
PSYCHIC DEFENSES

JEWELS OF PROTECTION

CHAPTER SEVEN

Whether you recently experienced a psychic attack or want to prevent one, ways to protect yourself from a psychic assault are relatively simple. There are a lot of psychic novels and teachers that state it takes a particular type of deity, ritual, and or crystals for proper protection. If a recommended practice works for you, keep doing it. However, if most of those suggestions you've encountered don't resonate, or you are looking for new tips and ideas, the good news is you can easily create your style in protecting your aura and yourself. The best part about owning your psychic powers is first accepting that these powers are yours and yours to do with them as you will. With great power comes great responsibility, but within that power comes taking and exploring your level of creativity. Each soul beholds his and her spark of wonder and everlasting glory. Within you is a mighty God or Goddess waiting to be unleashed through the gift of permission. This is where the fun begins for you, finally given a chance to embrace your fullest potential and harness your power on the right-hand path.

THE PROTECTION TYPES

Whether you're a beginner or advanced, it's crucial to understand the different levels of protection. As there are different types of attacks, there will always be distinct levels of security. The measures to protect one's aura from negative residual energy won't be the same as shielding from a metaphysical attack by an evil spirit. As the saying goes, the more aggressive the assault calls for more robust protection. Each type of protection shields, and crystals defend different parts of your astral body (soul), aura, mental/ emotional health, and physical body. The crystal's properties are also a guide when choosing the right crystal for the appropriate effects. It's essential to keep in mind these types are not meant to be used in the orders listed but are presented as a helpful tool and guide for another psychic defense.

CRYSTAL PROTECTION

Crystals have been widely known for centuries to possess outstanding amounts of healing properties, psychic benefits, and protection. It's as if mother earth knew they would come in handy for those who need it most. Crystals have been used to bring good health and fortune and even enhance one's psychic powers and magickal rituals through the ages as old as ancient Egyptian times. By simply wearing a crystal upon one's neck, wrist in the form of a bracelet, or as a ring, psychic properties and benefits from the crystals begin their work immediately. One of the main reasons crystals are in such high demand is that it's one of the easier tricks in psychic protection and empowerment.

Below is a list of the primary protection crystals that every Psychic, and Sensitive should have. It's unnecessary to go out of your way and buy every crystal, especially with how costly crystals have become. If you have that kind of financial freedom, go for it! However, if you're under a budget and only want ones that are the best at protection, this list has just that. Having just a few on your person can make all the magickal difference in securing your psychic defense. When choosing the suitable crystals for you, it's best to listen to your intuition and feel which one(s) you're the most drawn towards. Your inner guidance knows best, so trust in your higher senses and pick the ones that withstand the test.

- **ONYX**
  Properties: Absorbs negative energy, creates a protective shield, protects against emotional and physical vitality, and builds inner strength and self-confidence.

- **HEMATITE**
  Properties: Helps to remain grounded, strong psychic and home protection, shields and strengthens the aura, blocks

psychic attacks, black magick protection, cloaking abilities, builds self-confidence, connects with Archangel Michael.

- **TIGER'S EYE (golden)**
  Properties: Blocks psychic attacks, psychic, and home protection, strengthens the aura, builds personal empowerment, Evil Eye protection, Black magick protection, great for bully protection for children and adults.

- **AMETHYST**
  Properties: Psychic and home protection, blocks psychic attacks, cleansing, transmutes negative energy to positive energy, repairs and heals the aura, Black magick protection.

- **BLACK TOURMALINE**
  Properties: Psychic and home protection, blocks psychic attacks, EMF protection, strengthens and repairs the aura and cleansing.

- **CLEAR QUARTZ**
  Properties: Cleansing, strengthens and regenerates the aura and transmutes negative energy to positive energy, emotional healing, and psychic protection.

- **SMOKY QUARTZ**
  Properties: Psychic and home protection, cleansing, and EMF protection.

- **BLACK OBSIDIAN**
  Properties: Powerful psychic and home protection, blocks psychic attacks, psychic vampire protection, Black magick protection, and cuts unwanted Etheric cords.

- **SELENITE**
  Properties: Selenite is excellent for grounding, crystal cleansings, aura cleansing, psychic and home protection, blocks psychic attacks, negative spirit protection, and Angel connection/ protection.

  *Selenite is a mineral, not a crystal. When cleansing this mineral/crystal, it's important not to get it wet. Water makes the Selenite mineral get soft, causing it to separate and fall apart. The great thing about Selenite is it doesn't need to be charged or cleansed. However, if you want to charge it, using sage, palo santo wood, or leaving it in the sunlight for an hour will do.

- **JET**
  Properties: Psychic protection, Evil Eye protection, blocks psychic attacks, negative spirit protection, Shamanic protection, Elemental protection, and transmutes negative energy to positive energy.

- **LABRADORITE**
  Properties: Black magick protection, psychic protection, cloaking abilities, guards against psychic stalkers, guards

against unwanted remote viewers, guards against astral travelers, protects against familiar spirits and elementals.

- **JADE**

  Properties: Jade helps in psychic protection, guards against unwanted psychic stalkers, negative spirit protection, stabilizes the personality and promotes self-sufficiency, soothes the mind, releases negative thoughts and emotions, and attracts good luck and friendship.

- **AMBER**

  Properties: Amber absorbs negative energy, shields the aura, psychic protection, promotes good luck, protection from evil, balance, safety, grounding, eliminates anxiety and fears, acquires patience and wisdom, balances emotions, and even soothes body aches.

- **FLUORITE**

  Properties: Promotes self-confidence and is said to attract good luck and wealth. It helps in psychic protection, psychic attacks, and external manipulation and cleanses the aura.

- **CITRINE**

  Properties: Transmutes negative energy to positive energy, grounding, psychic, and home protection, transforming negative thoughts and emotions to positive ones.

- **APACHE TEAR**
  Properties: Psychic vampire protection, blocks psychic attacks, Astral attacks, raises awareness when recognizing dangerous situations, people, negative spirit protection, and gives emotional and mental security.

- **TURQUOISE**
  Properties: Helps in psychic protection, blocks psychic attacks, transmutes negative energy to positive energy, Evil Eye protection, Black magick protection, and raises intuition.

- **BLUE KYANITE**
  Properties: Connects to Archangel Michael, helps in psychic protection, blocks psychic attacks, mental and emotional defense, repels negative energy (and maybe your crazy ex - just kidding!) It builds and strengthens boundaries and cleanses both you and your aura.

- **DRAGON'S EYE**
  Properties: Powerful psychic and home protection, psychic attacks, Evil Eye protection, and Black magick protection.

- **FIRE AGATE**
  Properties: Protects from the Evil Eye, powerful psychic protection, Black magick protection, raises one's vibrations and is suitable for Starseeds.

- **GARNET**
  Properties: Blocks psychic attacks, bad luck, nightmare protection, psychic vampire protection, strong psychic protection, and gives aura cleansing.

- **GOLD SHEEN OBSIDIAN**
  Properties: Gives empowerment and confidence, psychic protection, mental and emotional protection, psychic attacks, and strengthens the aura.

- **GOLDSTONE**
  Properties: This gentle stone releases comfort to the wearer while giving psychic protection, EMF protection, and protects against psychic attacks. Good for children.

- **RUBY**
  Properties: Protects against psychic vampires, regenerates the aura, helps protect against psychic attacks, and builds confidence.

- **TIBETAN BLACK QUARTZ**
  Properties: Powerful psychic and home protection, guards against psychic attacks, cleansing, strengthens the aura, and transmutes negative energy to positive energy.

HOW TO USE CRYSTALS FOR PROTECTION

Knowing which crystal, when, and how to use it appropriately can be challenging and even intimidating at first. But this is an exciting experience when you allow the crystal to do its magick with trust in mother nature's treasures. Using the crystals can be done in nearly countless ways. It doesn't necessarily matter how one uses the crystal for it to do its job; all that matters is your will to believe in its energy benefits in good faith. Believing in the power of crystals is just as important as finding the right one. If one lacks trust in the jewel's psychic properties, it can backfire and even block from the person and not even work at all. All that truly matters is your trust and allow them to perform to protection.

If you're looking for new ways to use the crystals, here are a few tips to help receive the most effective defense and support daily.

- Wear crystal jewelry: necklaces, bracelets, earrings, rings, etc. Some believe the least dominant hand is the side where negative energy and entities will attach to you the most. So, if your left hand is dominant, wear rings or bracelets on your right hand or wrist. Vice versa if you're right-handed.

- Place crystals under or within your pillowcase or under the main bed sheet to protect against harmful spirits, astral kidnappings, psychic attacks, negative attachments, unwanted astral travel, etc.

- Place a crystal under your mattress or bed frame directly underneath your body when sleeping to protect against demonic entities and harmful spirits. Spirits like to creep underneath the sleeping living person to cling to their physical body and conduct psychic attacks.

- Wear crystals when you're around psychic vampires or when involved in unfamiliar situations with unfamiliar people.

- Carry a crystal attached to your car keys, purse, hat, backpack, satchel, suitcase, in your vehicle, or your wallet when going into the world full of the mundane. You don't want negative attachments or attacks.

- Wear certain crystals that heighten and strengthen your ability to say 'no' when in possible dangerous or unwanted situations and scenarios. Empaths, you know who you are.

- Crystals in your lap, held in your hands, or wearing crystals during meditation amplifies one's self-confidence, psychic protection, aura shielding, awakening/ connecting with the Higher Self, and connecting with Spirit Guides, Angels, Ascended Masters, etc.

- Create crystal grids. Crystal grids are a form of geometric spiritual patterns used to summon positive energy and protection. There are loads of helpful tips on the internet and books on using and making the best grids for the right intended barrier. If guided, you can also make your custom crystal grid through the guidance of your intuition, heart chakra, and Spirit Guides.

- Create crystal barriers. Crystal barriers are made by placing protection crystals at specific places of the home or location. For example, crystals placed near or at the front and back doors and windows will help protect against anyone who means harm, like Psychic Vampires and other opposing forces. The crystals quickly detect psychic energy and will work in one's favor immediately when the crystal senses a hostile wave.

CLEANSING AND CHARGING CRYSTALS

It's always important to consider who and how many people may have touched the crystal in the past. When purchasing a crystal, it would be wise to evaluate it when holding it in your hand. By observing and sensing the energetic signals from the crystal, one can quickly know when the crystal may have been tainted. Sometimes crystals handled by previous owners or prior customers can emit an energy that may not resonate well. When a person simply holds a crystal for a mere few seconds, their power can attach to that object. Although bound by their spiritual intentions, crystals can still be a victim of exposure to toxicity. When a person has had a bad day or is a psychic vampire, that prior person's energy quickly contaminates the crystal's aurific field. This can damage the crystal's work, so it's crucial in performing a sacred cleansing.

Whether cleansing 1 to 888 crystals, the positive charging process is still the same. Now, this is where I'm supposed to say, "There's no right or wrong way to charge your crystals" -on the contrary. The left-hand path is called the left-hand path for a reason, as it's considered the exact opposite of what is morally right. In this section, it's important to emphasize that proper cleansing is based on one's intentions. If you intend to bring in positive vibrations to purify the crystal of all harmful and toxic energy, then it's the right way. However, if you were stripped down to your birthday suit and smothered in sheep's blood and calling on to a demonic deity for it to cleanse your crystals, that's a cause for concern and in need of a spiritual intervention. Cleansing aims to integrate your positive intentions and the universal force with the highest good to purify the object, land, or people. However, this sacred ritual permits the energies to harmonize, and trans mutate negative energy. In this case, it's imperative to choose the purification wisely, even with crystals.

Below is a brief list of tips on how to efficiently cleanse and charge your crystals with the right intentions. When cleansing occurs, negative vibrations change into positive energy, thus enabling the crystal to be successfully charged for your protection and psychic wellbeing.

- Place the crystal(s) in the sun for at least an hour or longer. The sun's rays work like a transcended sun shower giving the crystals a supercharge. This also works well when working with the ancient Egyptian sun God Ra.

- Place your crystal(s) in a clean bowl of water, preferably purified, and place them in the sun for at least an hour. The longer they are in the sun, the better.

- Wash the crystal(s) in clean water with a pinch of salt. You can do this with or without salt; however, salt holds many purification properties used in many rituals and exorcisms.

- Cleanse the crystal(s) with White Sage. When doing so, it's essential to visualize and command that all negative energy be transitioned to positive vibrations for the good of your aura and temporary vessel.

- Cleanse the crystal(s) with Palo Santo wood. Palo Santo has powerful protection potential that is sacred in Native American purification rituals and other ancient civilizations. With the Palo Santo, you can ask the smoke to do its magick by protecting and harmonizing the crystal(s).

- Place your crystal(s) in a jar or bowl, with or without water, and place them under a Full or New Moon. The Full Moon is a time of releasing negative energy and emotions. The New Moon is about bringing in positive and new changes. Both moon phases would do well in charging and cleansing your crystal(s) like a spiritual makeover. Leave it under the moon overnight as soon as the moon is visible. Allow the moon's glistening glow to reprogram your gems in good faith that the universe has your back.

- Place your crystals near or touching a Selenite mineral crystal. Selenite has this unique gift of not needing to be recharged or cleansed that greatly benefits cleansing your crystal babies. Instead, leave the crystals next to the Selenite for at least an hour to allow the Selenite's aura to permeate the crystals with practical benevolence.

- You can call on Angels, Spirit Guides, Ancestors, benevolent Gods, and Goddesses to help you cleanse and charge your crystals. The powerful deities are an immense high vibration that can be highly beneficial. When doing so, request their assistance in humility with gratitude for their service and loving support.

- You can cleanse and charge the crystal with your God and Goddess particle for those in the magickal practice. Every person on earth is gifted with an enormous wealth of energy by the powerful universe. It becomes like mystical programming by taking the crystal and visualizing the universal energy surging through you and into the crystal. Programing a crystal is a light spell intended for the highest good and the most beneficial psychic intentions. In silence and uninterrupted focus, speak the desired intentions you want the crystal to do for you. When doing so, begin to imagine the upmost powerful thing you desire and believe in good faith that it's working. When you are done, thank the universe for the energy boost and yourself for your power and love, for you are the universe in human form.

WHEN TO CHARGE AND CLEANSE CRYSTALS (HOW OFTEN)

Whenever you feel your crystal(s) need an energetic charging, it's never a bad idea to give them some love. Like flowers make us smile, rejuvenated crystals help our aura brighten to its purest posture of perfection and psychic protection. You may be asking yourself, *"How often should I cleanse and charge my crystals?"* -Cleanse them at least once a month or as often as you feel guided. Like anything else, crystals need a good wash now and then to give back their shine and a helpful powerful push. Whenever cleansing and charging a crystal, do so with gratitude while visualizing the purification. By doing so, you're showing and bestowing love to one of earth's jewels.

CRYSTAL CAUTION

As beautiful as many mother earth gems are, some can be toxic. Malachite, for example, is not a crystal I recommend to anyone, for its poisonous and can even cause death if met with overexposure. In addition, some of the crystals suggested by psychics have led me to further disappointment due to their lack of research and safety concerns. Malachite can be worn if crafted within the safety regulations; however, not all crystal sellers will stick to these precautions, and many may not even be aware. Therefore, it's essential to always do your research on the crystals before buying them, wearing them, selling, or even gifting them to those you love. The last thing you'd want is to purchase a deadly addition to your wardrobe or protection collection.

Lastly, crystals should be guarded in every sense of the word. As one would be protective of their lover, child, best friend, or favorite ice cream, so should you be with your crystals. Crystals worn by others and then given back to you aren't necessarily good due to the continuous memory change of the crystal. If one considers the crystals like technology, the crystal becomes accustomed to your aura, thus will know when to work best in your favor. If you were to give the crystal to another rather too often, it might not harmonize with your frequency as it did before. Call me superstitious -still, personally, I'd instead not share any of my crystals with a "negative Nancy". Energy from another person can alter the state of the programming and can even backfire on your aura without warning. So, in this case, it's best to smile and tell your friend politely you'd instead buy them one of their own or recommend a crystal shop while secretly being just as protective of your crystal as they are of you. If you don't like sharing underwear with another, then I wouldn't go sharing your psychic protection gear -just don't do it.

SYMBOLS OF PROTECTION

When conducting a sense of psychic security, your person and your home are most important. Protection symbols have been used since ancient times. For example, some of the more prevalent signs like the Christian cross are copies of the ancient Egyptian cross Ankh which represents the *Egyptian sun God Ra*. All ancient civilizations and their religions had symbols with their own intention to protect and honor those in the benevolent power. Each deity assigned to the symbols establishes an understanding to the universe that you are being divinely guided, covered, and loved by the God and Goddess it depicts. Whether you are a Christian exploring the new age of the old ways, a Witch, a Wiccan, or a Psychic, these symbols will help protect against dark and malevolent forces. The provided symbols are listed to assist in finding additional security and divine protection. You don't need all the symbols to be psychically secure. If you are drawn to more than one symbol, listen to your divine message receiver (intuition). Next to each symbol is identifying the deity it is connected to.

ANKH

The Ankh is the ancient Egyptian symbol for the sun God Ra (Rah). Anyone who wears this symbol will receive divine protection and benevolent guidance from this ancient deity, the father of all ancient Egyptian Gods. Ra is also

considered the primary God, often depicted as the Light Bringer of Life and Creation in the Holy Bible. He is a bright light God full of immense power fueled by love and duality. His passion and guidance will significantly benefit one seeking spiritual warfare protection and psychic evolution.

THE TYET (THE KNOT OF ISIS)

The Tyet is the ancient Egyptian symbol for the Goddess Isis. Isis is the wife of the Divine Masculine God Osiris and is the mother of the God Horus. Isis is a Divine Feminine Master and Goddess, protecting women, children, and those in need of healing during childbearing. She helps the dead enter the afterlife and is considered one of the more powerful deities. Her maternal aid will help women looking to build their confidence, self-worth, and inner guidance towards the divine feminine. Isis is often glamoured in gold, red, and other precious gems. One of her many high qualities is her ability to guide and protect those seeking to secure their personal space, self-love, and spiritual warfare.

THE EYE OF HORUS

This symbol is connected to the ancient Egyptian Divine Masculine God Horus. Horus is the son of the God Osiris and Goddess Isis and is often depicted as a sky God due to his appearance as a human man with the head of a falcon. Those who wear the sign of Horus will receive the utmost divine guidance and protection. Being also the God of war, he will protect those in spiritual warfare and matters of physical threats. Horus is often seen as a man with a falcon head or as a man with dark hair, dark eyes draped in gold, gems, glistening in blue and green linen.

THE CAT OF BASTET

The ancient Egyptians are best known for worshipping cats, but few know where and why this came to be. Bastet, the ancient Egyptian Goddess, is the Divine Feminine deity connected to this Egyptian phenomenon. Bastet is the daughter of the Sun God Ra and has been known for many roles. She is best known as the protectress of women and children and assists during childbirth, warfare, perfume, and cats. One would see her as a woman with a feline body and cat head. Her Divine wisdom, tolerance, spiritual warfare experience, and mystery make her one of the more respected and admired deities.

THE HORNS OF HATHOR

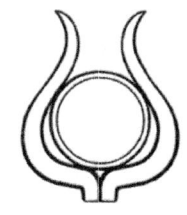

This Egyptian symbol represents the Divine Feminine Goddess Hathor. Hathor is often depicted as a cow, symbolizing her maternal and celestial instincts; however, she is often identified as a beautiful woman wearing cow horns and a sun disk upon her head. Hathor is best known as the divine counterpart to the Ancient God Horus and is one of the Feminine goddesses who acts as the Eye of Ra. Those who seek protection from Hathor would receive spiritual guidance, Divine Feminine support, and confidence. In addition, Hathor's ancient celestial powers are known to cross between worlds, helping both the living and deceased souls.

THE CRESCENT MOON

The Crescent Moon is one of the more popular among Witches, Wiccans, Psychics, Mediums and Pagans. This is because the crescent moon links one to the mysterious and acceptance of the universe and assists in psychic protection.

THE TRIPLE GODDESS MOON

The triple moon is linked to the creative power of the Mother Goddess. Witches and Wiccans drawn to this symbol will receive divine guidance from the Moon Goddess and magickal support for their craft. This symbol is also known to protect one from Psychic vampires, hexes, curses, and other psychic attacks.

THE PENTAGRAM

The Pentagram, or Pentacle, is a geometric symbol of intersecting lines, creating five-pointed ends that form a star. Each of the five points represents the elements of nature: Earth, Air, Fire, Water, and Spirit. This mathematical ratio was first recognized by the Greek mathematician Pythagoras. This symbol is used and most recognized by Witches, Wiccans, and Pagans. The Pentagram is known to help assist in spells and psychic protection from psychic vampires, psychic attacks, and negative vibrational entities. This symbol is also used during rituals to enhance one's magickal intentions.

THE OM

The meaning of the 'Om,' 'Ohm,' or 'Aum' is a sacred sound best known as the sound of the universe. The Om is considered a holy symbol in Indic religions. Its meaning and connotations vary between diverse and personal interpretations within the various traditions. One would find Om in Hinduism, Buddhism, Jainism, and Sikhism. Om is all-encompassing, the essence of ultimate reality, and unifies everything in the universe. Om is often used to symbolize protection, harmony, and purity.

THE HAMSA

The hand of Hamsa is derived from the word "Hamesh," which is connected to Hebrew origin, which means five (5). This symbolizes good luck, prosperity, faith, and riches. This symbol is also often used to ward off evil spirits with the "Evil Eye" protection, ensuring the safety of psychic attacks on those who wear this symbol. Originally, Hamsa served as a protection against ghosts and other evil spirits.

THE EVIL EYE

The Evil Eye is a supernatural belief that an evil glare can bring a curse or a hex, dating back to ancient Greece. This hex or curse can bring severe affliction by directing a look toward an unaware person. This old belief is as strong today, especially among those in energy work and magick. Those who wear the Evil Eye do so intending to protect against hexes, curses, psychic attacks, astral attacks, psychic vampires, evil spirits, and bad luck.

THE HEPTAGRAM

This symbol is known among neopagans as the Elven Star or Fairy Star. It is considered a sacred symbol in various modern Pagan and Witchcraft traditions. Blue Star Wicca also uses the symbol, where it's referred to as a Septagram.

The Heptagram is important in Western Kabbalah, where it symbolizes the spheres of Netzach, the seven planets, the seven alchemical metals, and the seven days of the week. The Heptagram symbolizes magickal power in various Pagan spiritualities and traditions. Those pulled to wear this symbol will benefit from protection seven days of the week and enhance one's spells in magick.

THE BIBLICAL CROSS

In Christian theology, the cross is defined as a symbol of God's self-sacrificing love (agape). Its vertical and horizontal axis represents the two central teachings of Jesus Christ (Yehoshua): the love of God and your neighbor. Whosoever chooses to wear this  symbol will benefit from Angelic protection and divine guidance from celestial benevolence. Although it appears like an Ankh copycat, their deities and identifications are the divine difference between them.

THE TRIQUETRA

The Triquetra is a triangular figure composed of three interlaced arcs. It is used as an ornamental design in architecture and medieval manuscript illumination. Within the Wiccan and Pagan traditions, the knotwork  is meant to shield one from evil. Some interpret the Triquetra as a symbol of connection between the body, mind, and soul. Some interpret the knotwork as representing the three realms of earth, sea, and sky. Wearing this symbol is meant to protect one from the evil of all the natural elements, including evil spirits.

THE CELTIC CROSS

The Celtic Cross consists of the five energy points: one sizeable central point surrounded by four Triquetra symbols. This symbol protects from physical, psychological, and psychic danger. In addition, this symbol creates a powerful energetic shield also protecting the wearer from psychic attacks.

THE PEACE SIGN

The Peace sign meaning remains alive and flourishing today. The sign represents harmony, union, and the focus of love, not war, as an ideal concept for the world. The Peace sign is not only worn by hippies but by those who firmly believe in the positive messages instilled into the symbol and its intentions. With faith in its meaning, those who wear this symbol will receive and bestow good luck, kindness, joy, love, and kinship with others. The sign also promotes benevolent protection.

THE SOLAR CROSS

The Solar Cross is intended as a protective symbol, evoking the Sun God or All-Father's power and the guardians of the Four Directions. As a centering power exercise, it is recommended to focus on the intersection of  the cross when meditating. This cross also represents balance (at its center) and infinity (at its extremities). When wearing the Solar Cross, one is better protected from malevolent forces and unwanted negative attachments thanks to the protective shield it creates.

THE STAR OF DAVID

The Star of David, also known as the Shield of King David -is a well-known Jewish symbol. This symbol is on the Israeli national flag as a sign of hope and protection for every Jew. The Star of David is also used by Christians, Hindus, and Muslims  independently. This powerful star is believed by many to protect one from the Evil Eye. It represents a rich religious history and is widely considered a proud symbol among the Jews and others alike.

ANGELIC SYMBOLS

Thanks to a wide variety of Angelic symbolism, one doesn't require a specific symbol per se when seeking Angel protection or guidance. Angels have a unique ability to hear our telepathic thoughts and prayers without the need for a  symbol. However, each Angel does have a special geometric symbol or sigil that is often used to summon, work, or seek their divine protection. One can acquire these angelic symbols from the internet or other helpful sources. Wearing a symbol like Angel wings, for example, can amplify one's protective energetic field. Simply calling on Angels for guidance, healing, and protection will build confidence and promote a lighter and positive attitude, thanks to the Angel's extensive healing capabilities and high vibrations.

THE PHOENIX

The Phoenix symbolizes death and rebirth and the immortality of the soul. The Phoenix is a legendary bird that is believed to have red and golden feathers and a beautiful voice like music. The origin of the understanding of the Phoenix comes from  ancient Greece and ancient Egypt. A phoenix's primary purpose is to promote protection against evil forces. It would forever escape death since its feathers would regrow. The symbol of the Phoenix also represents death and resurrection from the ashes.

Anyone who was to pray to the Phoenix or wear a symbol of this remarkable bird would gain psychic protection, specifically of a fiery shield. Aries, Leo, and Sagittarius would benefit significantly with the help of this fire deity and its otherworldly wonder.

THE DRAGON

Since ancient China, the Dragon spirit has been a treasured yet feared deity by all who encounter it. The Dragon spirit has been worshipped and veered as a divine protector against demons, devils, and psychic attacks. Those lucky enough to meet these spirits are in for an awe-inspiring awakening. Dragons are more extensive than any creature known in the ethereal world and have unique and great powers shared with those blessed to receive the experience and bond with these beautiful creatures. Dragons are mighty beings that are feared for their greatness and supernatural wealth. Wearing a dragon symbol or having dragon art on the walls of one's home will be blessed by the psychic protection of the dragons.

CLEANSING AND CHARGING SYMBOLS

Some believe you don't need to purify a protective symbol; however, negative energy can attach to objects, as we covered before. Cleansing and charging your protective symbols will be like the tips suggested for crystals. When a symbol is connected to a specific Spirit, it's beneficial to call onto the deity and humbly ask for the spirit to bless your object with their benevolent protection surge. During this blessing, remember to thank the kind spirit for their time and the purification of their loving shield. This process shouldn't take longer than a few minutes, for spirits are not bound by earth time and can do so within seconds.

Every piece of protection comes with one's personal preference and pull towards what works for you. Thankfully if even this list does not suffice your psychic appetite, there are other countless trusted sources. Wearing crystals and protective symbols when leaving your home or during a stressful time benefits your aura and mental health. Protection symbols depicting a specific deity not only will protect you without question in many scenarios but will assist in your psychic confidence when sensing potential threats and evil otherworldly forces.

HIGH DEFENSE AND PURIFICATION

CHAPTER EIGHT

Securing one's safety is not always easy, especially after experiencing a psychic affliction. I won't lie to you. There will be moments where you will feel insecure in your psychic capabilities. You may even now doubt your ability to protect against an unruly foe. If ever in doubt, know that to proceed regardless of the situation is where your true power will lie. True power is within one's purest intentions and desires to protect and deflect against those who mean you harm. Even if you consider yourself a newborn in the realm of unlimited consciousness and psychic potential, you're still more powerful at this moment than you could ever imagine. Every part of your metaphysical being has been craving for this moment. Although one's level of experience can indeed measure the light bearer's infinite potential, that doesn't mean you're not already on the way to unlocking your God Particle of supreme protection. Once your inner Divinity has been unleashed, the need for the following list of defense and purification will be needed less frequently. As one ascends into their God Particle, the need for earthly materials for metaphysical protection will no longer be a necessity. But there are ways to establish heavy-duty shields for your aura, physicality, and home until then.

The jewels of unwavering healing, protection, and grounding can only do so much, so this portion will help those looking for other ways of high vibrational defense and purification. The list of psychic tips, methods, and deities will not only ensure added safety from hostile energies and entities but will heal and amplify your aura and psychic power. Every item and ritual mentioned will boost your defense and counteract any attacks sent to you. The psychic energy sent with hostility will be deflected and blocked, which will create a magickal forcefield of protection.

Each defense method is highly recommended by the guidance of the Ascended Masters, Angels, and Spirit Guides. Listen to your intuition when picking which ways are best for you. Allow your intuition to guide you toward the methods that will work the best with you in trust in your Higher Self. This is your time to shine and get control back into your life! Whether you're looking to cleanse from a previous attack, prevent a psychic attack, reverse a curse or a hex, or counter and banish a hostile spirit etc., you'll find that each method benefits all needs.

WHITE SAGE

White sage is an herb that can be purchased online and at new age and crystal shops. Sage is an herb that burns like incense. Sage can be burned in the bundle or broken into pieces on a safe burning dish or bowl.

Metaphysical Benefits:
Sage will transmute all negative energy into positive vibrations. This remarkable yet powerful herb will help balance emotions, chakras, grounding during meditation, yoga, etc.

How to Use:
It is always recommended to sage your bedroom first or wherever you feel needs it most. When you begin the cleansing, cleanse indoors with your windows open to push OUT the negativity. Do NOT cleanse outside first and then inside, for this will force the negative energies and spirits to be locked inside the home/ land. When you begin, safely burn the bundle of sage like you would an incense stick in your hand or broken into pieces on a safe burning plate, cauldron, or bowl. When the flame has burned enough of the sage bundle to one's judgment, safely blow out (extinguish) the fire. When the sage smoke begins to spread, safely and slowly waft the smoke toward areas you feel need to be cleansed of negative energy. This process will cleanse you and your home simultaneously. Wafting the smoke with a feather of your choice is customary but not required.

*Burn away from children, pets, wind, potential drafts, and hazardous chemicals and items that will catch fire. Do not leave it unattended when burning.

When to Use:
Burn sage whenever you sense negative energy or an evil spirit. Sage will not banish evil spirits like Demons or Devils -however, it will intensely cleanse your aura, astral body, and physical body from hostile energies.

FRANKINCENSE

Frankincense is an aromatic resin from Boswellia trees used in incense and perfumes. Frankincense can also be found in candles, incense sticks, and incense cones.

Metaphysical Benefits:
It will help with clearing negative emotions, energies, and evil spirits. Helps protect against psychic attacks and psychic vampires. Builds psychic shields and helps connect with Spirit Guides and Higher Self. Powerful against Demons, Devils, and other evil spirits.

How to Use:
Frankincense can be burned like Sage on a safe burning plate, bowl, or cauldron. When burning the Frankincense, carry the

smoky resin to every room of your home and location if desired to cleanse negative energies and entities.

*Burn away from children, pets, wind, potential drafts, and hazardous chemicals and items that will catch fire. Do not leave it unattended when burning.

When to Use:
The best time to use Frankincense is when you feel the most threatened by unfriendly spirits or negative vibrations. This resin is also commonly used in exorcisms and Banishment.

MYRRH

Myrrh is a gum-resin extracted from several small trees' species of the genus Commiphora. It is commonly used as a spiritual incense and medicine. Myrrh is used as magick candles, incense sticks, and incense cones. Frankincense is often paired with Myrrh because of its powerful properties and the complimentary smell when combined.

Metaphysical Benefits:
Myrrh transmutes negative energies, emotions, and thoughts. Balances chakras and helps in grounding. Builds psychic boundaries and amplifies one's psychic connection with Spirit Guides and Higher Self.

How To Use:
This resin can be burned in the same way as Sage and Frankincense.

*Burn away from children, pets, wind, potential drafts, and hazardous chemicals and items that will catch fire. Do not leave it unattended when burning.

When to Use:
When experiencing a psychic attack or cleansing from a previous episode or psychic vampires. Myrrh is commonly used in exorcisms and Banishment.

PALO SANTO

Palo Santo is a medicinal tree that grows in numerous exotic places, including the Galapagos Islands, Argentina, Bolivia, and Ecuador. Palo Santo wood is commonly found in crystal/ new age/ occult shops online.

Metaphysical Benefits:
Palo Santo wood, or "holy wood," enhances one's spiritual experiences and clears negative energy, and defends against evil spirits. They are commonly added in exorcisms, Banishment of hexes, curses, negative people, and situations.

How To Use:
This holy wood burns just like an incense stick. When ready, safely burn the Palo Santo stick in your hand. Let the wood burn for a few seconds, just long enough to get the tip of the stick red hot. Upon your safe judgment, blow out (extinguish) the flame. Once the flame has gone out, the smoke will trail from the Palo Santo, similar to an incense stick. During this moment, at a safe distance, trail the Palo Santo stick around you in a giant circle and visualize the blessing and cleansing of the holy wood. Then patiently bless your home with the Palo Santo incense by entering every house room with the stick in hand. Slowly wave the stick into every corner of each room. You can also bless each room by trailing the smoke in the form of a circle.

*Burn away from children, pets, wind, potential drafts, and hazardous chemicals and items that will catch fire. Do not leave it unattended when burning.

When to Use:
Palo Santo is best used before and after Paranormal Investigations, harmful paranormal activity, psychic attacks, when around psychic vampires, and unhappy/ negative situations.

LAVENDER

As nature holds its power source, so are the flowers that bloom. Lavender is a potent and favorable herb used in protection and healing.

Metaphysical Benefits:
The powerful scent promotes emotional wellness, healing, and mental stability and negates negativity. In addition, it creates a shield of protection and purification through aromatherapy and spell work.

How to Use:
Because Lavender is so quickly versatile, one can use this magickal property in nearly countless ways. The healing power from this flower can be harnessed through tea, lotion, bath salt, bath soaps, shampoo, and conditioner, as a resin, coupled with sage bundles, essential oils, candles, and incense. Again, Lavender can be used in so many ways, making it fun and easy to find what resonates with you. When using Lavender for what you seek to manifest, it's essential to focus on the purpose and intention.

When to Use:
Use when you feel negative energy is surrounding you, a harmful spirit is near, or you think you've been around a psychic vampire. Lavender is also best used to cleanse stressful situations and

emotional happenings. Lavender is also used to clear negative thoughts and feelings and for good luck.

SANDALWOOD

Sandalwood is believed to hold a strong connection with exceptional spiritual properties. This sacred wood heightens one's spiritual connection with the ethereal realms, the divine, and their Higher Self. This is also considered one of the more powerful woods used in protection and exorcisms.

Metaphysical Benefits:
Sandalwood heals the aura, cleansing from negative residual energy, and establishes a bountiful high vibration within your Higher Self. This expensive and high-demand wood ignites an energetic barrier of protection, healing, and metaphysical security.

How to Use:
Sandalwood is often used in incense sticks, incense cones, as a stick, or as a resin that can be burned. Sandalwood also comes as an essential oil used in candle magick to clear any unholy energy and entities. Some people prefer to use Sandalwood when intending to connect with their Higher Self, Spirit Guides, Ascended Masters, Ancestors, Elementals, and other Divine deities.

When to Use:
This unique wood is best used when you feel psychically threatened and command peace, safety, healing, and security in your aura and home.

LEMONGRASS

Lemongrass is a tropical grass that yields an oil that smells of lemon -hence the name. It's widely used in Asian dishes, medicine, perfumes, and herbal teas.

Metaphysical Benefits:
Lemongrass is believed to bring good luck and protect against evil. Some find healing through this high vibrational plant that dispels terrible luck and harmful attachments and aids in situational roadblocks. Lemongrass is considered a road opener and renewal for positive outcomes and abundance.

How to Use:
One can use Lemongrass in many ways, including but not limited to herbal teas, skin-safe essential oils, potions, spells, and protection magick. Because of the plant's high vibration, it will help in clearing negative attachments, chakra blockages, and bad luck. When Lemongrass is used, it raises your vibration, thus enabling your aura to become high vibrational, making it easier to ward off evil and harmful energies.

When to Use:
Use when you feel something negative is blocking your path to success and abundance. Also, it is best to use it whenever your vibration is low, and you need to heal from toxic past experiences, unsettling emotions, psychic vampires, and hostile spirits.

DRAGON'S BLOOD

Dragon's Blood is a bright red resin obtained from several different species of plants. The ruby-like resin has been used since ancient times in medicine, like a varnish, as incense and dye.

Metaphysical Benefits:
Dragon's Blood benefits include healing negative and hostile situations and enriching the astral body into the Higher Self. The resin brings protection from negative energy, wicked people and concerns, and evil spirits. Dragon's Blood also helps in connection with the Dragon Spirits. As it associates with fire energy, the powerful properties of Dragon's Blood are especially beneficial to astrological fire signs: Leo, Aries, and Sagittarius. This is because they have fire in their astrological chart. Dragon's Blood creates a mighty barrier of protection. This resin is also used in banishments of negativity, commanding clearing of toxic people, situations, bad luck, breaking curses, hexes, and exorcisms.

How to Use:
Dragon's Blood is commonly used and sold as an incense stick, incense cone, resin powder, Sage coated in Dragon's Blood, essential oil, magick candles, etc. When cleansing and Banishing, visualize all the negativity vanishing from your aura and protecting you from hostile forces. The power of Dragon's Blood can be used when invoking and evoking Dragon Spirits during protection magick. Dragon Spirits are incredibly skilled in aiding in shielding others and helping in establishing a sacred space because, let's face it, no one wants to mess with a dragon.

When to Use:
When a person means business, they use Dragon's Blood. Use when you feel your safety and mental wellbeing is being threatened. This is especially powerful against Demonic entities, Devils, and other familiar spirits. It's highly spiritually advised to use Dragon's Blood when you feel intuitively drawn toward its spiritual protection properties and healing benefits.

WHITE SALT

White salt protection is commonly used and is highly favored among Witches, Wiccans, Psychic Mediums, and Lightworkers. Whether one uses simple table salt or natural sea salt -the proactive metaphysical properties work the same.

Metaphysical Benefits:
White Salt is best for securing a protective barrier from outside hostile energies, spirits, situations, and people. Whosoever means you harm, cannot cross this barrier of protection. Some believe natural sea salt carries more bountiful benefits, but regular table salt is equally mighty.

How to Use:
Sprinkle lines of white salt around your entire property to ensure metaphysical protection. If you don't want or can't afford that much salt, you can also sprinkle lines of white salt in front of doors entering the home and in front of windows. When doing so, visualize a strong shield that is now protecting you and your property. This is also helpful when purposefully keeping away stalkers, ex-lovers, and anyone you don't want to enter or come near your home.

When to Use:
Make white salt barriers every few months to every few weeks. As one enters and exits the home, opens, and closes windows -not to forget the happenings of weather, the salt will break away over time, so be sure to recreate the white salt barrier as needed. Creating a white salt barrier will promote positive energy and ward off malignant forces intending to harm. If you experience nightmares or what seems like demonic night terrors (attacks); make a white salt barrier around your bed. This will also help in protecting against unwanted astral visitors and astral attacks.

BLACK SALT

Black salt is explicitly crafted to ward off negative people, unwanted situations, negative energies, and evil spirits. Black salt is commonly mistaken for Black Magick because of its color difference from typical white salt. However, as everything in magick is made with the intention of the desired outcome, the color is used to represent the undesirable but is far from Black Magick. Witches of the "white craft" or "good" witches also concoct Black salt for protection.

Metaphysical Benefits:
This particular salt is made to shield against negative and hostile forces, people, situations, bad luck, curses, hexes, evil spirits, and unwanted attachments. This is especially helpful in keeping certain people away from you, your home, and even 'bumping into you.' Witches often use Black salt whenever they feel their security is threatened and banish unwanted situations, psychic attacks, enemies, etc.

How to Use:
Black Salt can be used in the same way as White Salt. The difference is Black Salt is specifically crafted with the witch's psychic and magickal intention to ward off specific people, situations, or spirits.

*If you purchase Black Salt from another witch, it's necessary to check the person doesn't work with unholy spirits like Demons, Devils, and other antagonistic deities. Those that work with evil forces will infuse the negative energy with the help of their deity into their craft. Also, the ingredients of Black Salt may vary and is not meant to be consumed.

When to Use:
Use Black salt when you intend to shield against those who mean you harm like stalkers, unfriendly neighbors, suspicious people, psychic vampires, negative people, negative situations, etc. Smile as you sprinkle this powerful dash of Black commandment because 'once you go black, you never go back' -to white table salt.

RED BRICK DUST
Red Brick Dust is often stated as a cross between vodou and hoodoo ritual by African American slaves that originated between the 1700's and 1800's. However, the protection of Red Brick Dust goes far back as thousands of years from ancient Greece, ancient Egypt, parts of Africa, and Europe. In some old practices, Red Brick Dust wasn't brick but a red ochre mineral. As years passed, this ancient shield's ingredients and protective measures adapted to a more modern and practical approach. Today Red Brick Dust is crafted by precisely what it's called -grounded red bricks and or other added ingredients.

Metaphysical Benefits:
Growing in popularity, it's understood and meant to protect one from harm, negative people, unwanted situations, and evil entities.

How to Use:
Sprinkle Red Brick Dust at the main entries of your home, in front of windows, at your business, or around your entire land. Brick dust can also be sprinkled around one's bed to protect against harmful spirits, uninvited astral travelers, and psychic attacks. It's essential to visualize and speak aloud what you wish this Dust to do in your favor through protection.

When to Use:
Brick Dust can be used the same as White and Black Salt. Use whenever you feel it is needed and how often you intuitively feel it is necessary.

HOLY WATER

Holy Water is blessed water popular among the Catholic Church by Priests and Exorcists. However, Holy Water doesn't need to be blessed by just those of a religious rite -anyone can make Holy Water! You don't need to get Holy Water approved by a church, nor should you have to pay for it! You can easily make your own Holy Water in the comfort of your own home.

Metaphysical Benefits:
Holy Water is used as protection that enforces a psychic cleansing, shields against negative spirits, and hostile energies, and is a destroyer of curses and hexes. In addition, Holy Water replenishes the aura as a source of healing and restoration from evil energy, emotions, and situations such as exorcism and Banishment.

How to Use:
All one will need is a glass, bowl, or spray bottle filled with purified spring water. Then, with a confident mind guided by faith, command the water to be blessed with your God Particle (power). You can also request in prayer for a deity of your choice that you trust to bless the water with their benevolent power. When the water is blessed, thank the kind spirit as you sprinkle, dash, or spray the blessed water on yourself, the property, and objects. Holy water can bless things one suspects may be cursed or carries negative residual energy or attachments. One can also add a pinch of white salt to infuse the Holy Water with an extra kick of positive vibrations *(ironically, priests often make holy water in the same as witches.)*

When to Use:
Bless yourself, your home, or your objects whenever you feel it is necessary. Not always are blessings going to work the first or even second time, which is why it's called spiritual warfare. But remain consistent and faithful that the good of the universe has your back!

TIBETAN SINGING BOWLS

A Tibetan Singing Bowl, also known as a Himalayan bowl, promotes powerful healing properties and spiritual relaxation. Buddhist monks have long used these richly deep-toned playing bowls in their meditation practice. However, it's not the bowl's sound that brings peace and relaxation but the vibrations these unique bowls give off. Singing bowls have been around for over 2,000 years and have become a widespread recommended sound therapy practice.

Metaphysical Benefits:
Singing bowls are commonly used to echo high vibrations in the space. The vibrations are believed to heal unsettling emotions, negative thoughts, anxiety, worry, and doubt. Tibetan Singing bowls are often used to clear away negative energies and evil spirits and harmonize those in the space to a positive vibration. They are also a favorite ritual before and or during yoga and meditation.

How to Use:
A Singing bowl comes with a mallet designed to gently tap or graze the singing bowl around the outside top edge of the bowl. The sound of a singing bowl is a harmonious sound giving off soothing vibrations to ease stress and an overly active mind. It can be used by tapping three times for a few seconds between each tap with the singing bowl mallet. Every Singing bowl comes in

different sizes and colors, and some will sound slightly different from others.

When to Use:
Listen to your intuition when using a singing bowl. Some people prefer to use the singing bowl daily in meditation or yoga, whereas others prefer to use it only a few times a month. There is no right or wrong time when using a singing bowl. It doesn't make a person more or less spiritual. However, if you feel the singing bowl works for you and brings you to a metaphysical divinity, then, by all means, enjoy the soothing singing bowl melody.

AQUATIC PURIFICATION

If you feel you are carrying an unsettling amount of negative residual energy or have recently survived a psychic attack or a psychic vampire, this may be perfect for you! Aquatic purification is especially helpful for Empaths and those with water in their chart or water astrological zodiac signs, Pisces, Cancer, and Scorpio. A Purification Shower or Bath is best for those needing to cleanse off their aura, astral body, and physical body from overexposure to negative people, situations, emotions, psychic attacks, psychic vampires, hexes, curses, evil spirits, stress, anxiety, or negative attachments.

Metaphysical Benefits:
A Purification Bath or Shower can have massive spiritual benefits, including raising one's vibration, clearing negative attachments, clearing negative emotions, clearing negative thoughts, and cleansing from psychic attacks.

How to Use:
All one needs is a solid psychic intention with your heart chakra and free will to purify with water. When in the shower or bathtub, visualize the water cleansing and clearing away any negative energy and making your aura brighter. During this therapeutic process, close your eyes as you say what you want the water to do with full intentions and command. Some people like to use their favorite essential oils during this process or skin-safe bath salts intended for cleansing. You don't need anything specific, but at least one type of soap you like while visualizing during the aquatic meditation that you're free from toxic vibrations. You can also do this cleansing in the glorious waves of your favorite beach with the benefits of the natural sea salt. As you step into the oceanic cosmic flow, ask the Mermaid spirits and other aquatic spirits to cleanse you of the toxins. Thank the water spirits for their generous support and love when you feel the cleansing is complete.

When to Use:
Do this aquatic purification process at least once a month or whenever you bathe. This spiritual cleansing process is meant to alleviate and wash away energy prone to linger like a metaphysical muck or muddy substance. Water isn't known as a purifier in many

religions by coincidence, as water is scientifically proven to heal and mend emotions through loving thoughts and intentions.

PSYCHIC FORCEFIELD OF PROTECTION
(MEDITATION FORCEFIELD)

It gets a little more advanced for those searching for a solid energetic barrier of psychic protection. A psychic forcefield is precisely how it sounds, a psychic protective barrier created by your focused thoughts and deep-rooted intentions. Whether you're looking to use this once in a while or daily, it can be done with the right emotional and mental balance. A psychic forcefield is an energetic protective barrier surrounding your entire being in any shape, color, and element that resonates with the psychic.

Metaphysical Benefits:
This psychic technique gives you a stronger sense of psychic protection from psychic vampires, curses, hexes, hateful thoughts, negative residual energy, evil spirits, and psychic attacks. It strengthens your aura while guarding against those who mean you harm.

How to Use:
During meditation, focus on visualizing a mighty bright and colorful forcefield surrounding your body and astral body while protecting your aura. The forcefield can be shaped and

manifested in any color, size, and design you prefer so much as long as it resonates with your Higher Self with positive intentions. The stronger your will, the more powerful it can become. If you need help in doing this, especially if it's your first time, ask your Spirit Guides and other ascended light beings to assist you. The more you do it, the easier it is, the faster it manifests, and the more glorious it will be. The more often you meditate and envision your aura of protection, you may even begin to feel a high level of vibrations surge through your body. Those that are more advanced and experienced in meditation often know when this occurs and how to control it.

When to Use:
Creating your psychic forcefield is best done when you know you require extra protection. Empaths, Psychics, Mediums, Witches, and Lightworkers will benefit significantly from this technique. Do so when you know your psychic wellbeing is threatened or when facing spiritual warfare.

PSYCHIC SHIELD OF PROTECTION
(ADVANCED PSYCHIC TECHNIQUE)

In spiritual warfare as a Lightwarrior, Lightworker, Demonologist (the study of demons -not worship), Paranormal Investigator, Exorcist, Witch, Psychic Medium, or avid Astral Traveler, this advanced psychic protection will serve you very well. I have contemplated sharing this piece of psychic information as I planned to save this for another future book. However, over time, I realized it was inadvertently appropriate and exceptionally needed! Many psychics express their desire to shield against a hostile force better psychically in the astral realm and other dimensions. A Psychic Shield of Protection is an energetic shield one creates with the powers of the mind and the use of the God Particle.

Metaphysical Benefits:
This shield is best used during astral combat or within the vast dimensions beyond time and space. When confronted by a demonic entity, devil, or other negative vibrational foes, this shield will become a part of your spiritual armor. It not only will shield against many psychic attacks but will counteract those attacks and send them back to the enemy simultaneously.

How to Use:
A psychic shield is manifested from a highly skilled and well-grounded magician, Psychic Medium, astral Lightwarrior, God, Goddess, Ascended Masters, Starseeds, and Angels. The psychic shield can only be manifested with intense focus and advanced meditation during combat. Those who have ascended to the 5th dimension and higher are more likely and can know and harness this psychic skill. If you're new to the psychic shield and want to craft this special protection successfully, it's best to ask for spiritual warfare training -and even then, you must know how to Astral Project on command to do so. This can take several years to master, but anyone can do it! Only those who have excelled in

their spiritual warfare training with Ascended Masters, Gods, and Goddesses are capable of producing a psychic shield. With the right amount of dedication, psychic training by your Spirit Guides, and enough Astral Combat under your belt, you will be able to conjure a psychic shield. Don't fret if you can't right away. As long as you believe you can and are patient in the learning process, you will become successful in your own time. One must believe you can do this and feel the power inside you. This isn't quickly produced and takes even the more experienced Psychics, Witches, and anyone sometimes a lifetime to master. It all depends on you and you alone.

If you are sure you're ready for this advanced training, it is advised to seek proper psychic training with trustworthy benevolent Spirit Guides knowledgeable in spiritual warfare. Archangels, Gods, Goddesses, Starseeds, and other Ascended Masters are some recommended guides.

When conducting a psychic shield, it's best to visualize in a peaceful meditative state with a lot of passion guided by the heart chakra. Protecting those you love or yourself from harm is the primary motivator that is the most valuable source of reason. As we are faced with immediate physical threats on earth, there are supernatural oppositions with aggressive intentions. When you feel and see your shield coming into manifestation, begin to shape the guard to your liking and in a color and size that brings you confidence.

I often make my shield bedazzled in colorful light and jewels. There is no limit to how you can make your shield of protection. All that matters is you believe you can, and once you do, there is no stopping you!

When to Use:
Use the shield when you are faced with supernatural danger. Manifest your shield when you feel your energy is being threatened. The psychic shield does not guarantee physical safety -obviously this is strictly a metaphysical psychic technique for otherworldly confrontations.

MAGICK PROTECTION

Protection through magick possesses endless possibilities within the intuition of the Witch. Magick is the ability and intention to manipulate and maneuver energy to one's benefit. Doing what resonates with your calling and aligns with your personality is vital when performing any ritual, spell, invocation, or evocation. Doing a spell that gives you the power to protect and deflect hostile energies should always resonate with your sense of Higher Self and inner God and Goddess. There is no right or wrong way how one creates psychic protection through magick as long as it's built and fueled through love, healing, and benevolence.

Metaphysical Benefits:
Magick conducted with respect and knowledge of the laws of karma will benefit the caster greatly. Magick is neither good nor evil as it depends on the manifester's core intentions and deepest desires. When a spell is crafted with the intention of psychic protection and wellbeing, the benefits can be tremendous and

nearly endless. The pros can lead to psychic protection against psychic vampires, bad luck, nightmares, psychic attacks, evil spirits, uninvited astral travelers, curses, hexes, etc. Magick can protect from illness and has the potential to cure illnesses, however magick should not replace medical and medicinal assistance by a licensed health practitioner.

How to Use:
Witches don't call it the 'craft' for nothing. You are the artist in your magick and can independently create your psychic shields and forcefields. Many Witches make shields through the elements of nature: fire, water, earth, and air. Other Witches cast protection magick with plants, herbs, spices, essential oils, flower gardens, meditation, or through fire and smoke using candle magick. The best part about magick is you can do what resonates with you. As long as you feel the power of protection working through your incantations and creations, then it will be.

When to Use:
Protection through magick should be used when you sense unfamiliar energy is near and is potentially harmful. Best to use when you know you're going to be near a psychic vampire, experience psychic attacks, have nightmares, encounter evil spirits, or want to avoid hostile people and situations. When attacked or threatened by a Black Magick Witch, Demonolater, or Devil worshipper, Magick protection is *highly* recommended.

ETHERIC CORD-CUTTING

Although we may remember to put on our seatbelts, a lot of us tend to forget where the emergency brake is and how to use it. Like when driving a vehicle, it's crucial to know how to make an emergency stop in risky and unexpected situations. Unfortunately, Etheric Cord Cutting is as important as the emergency brake but is often forgotten. As we develop relationships with people, spirits, and people we just met can often make etheric attachments. This cord is much like a metaphysical umbilical cord connection between you and another person. These cords can be commonly made through lovers, best friends, siblings (especially twins), family members, pets, and children. An etheric attachment or cord can be linked between you and someone else either intentionally or obliviously. One doesn't have to make an etheric cord consciously to create one knowingly. As long as there's an exceptionally powerful emotional attachment or bond, that link is often synced between two partners.

As humans and departed human spirits can create attachments, so can demons, devils, and many other evil entities. Therefore, ensuring your psychic safety by managing unwanted etheric extensions is a must! One can develop mild to severe health symptoms without asserting awareness of this threat.

How to Use:

Cutting an Etheric attachment or cord must be done by an experienced metaphysical practitioner. A Reiki Master can do this, Psychic Medium, Witch, Wiccan, Wizard, or benevolent Spirit Guides skilled in detachments. If you cannot find anyone who can do an etheric cord cut, you can pray to Archangel Michael, Archangel Gabriel, or any Angel you trust capable of this task. Not all Angels and Spirit Guides are trained in cord-cutting like an Archangel or other ascended Angels, so it's best to do your research before making such a request.

When to Use:

If you ever feel like you have a negative attachment and want the etheric cord cut, there is never a better time than now! Get it done as soon as possible! The sooner you can cut a harmful attachment, the lesser the chance of severe health complications soon -if not experienced already.

DIVINE DEITY DEFENSE

As you develop your psychic awareness and acquire other talents with your abilities, you're bound to attract unwanted attention. As I've stated initially, negative vibrational spirits are not *only* attracted to negative vibrational people, situations, locations, or circumstances. They can and are often drawn toward people of a higher vibration level that gives off an even brighter light through their psychic energy. The more advanced you grow in your abilities and psychic ascension, the more you become a dazzling target. When negative entities are dim in their power and are low in vibration, your higher and brighter shine gain attention to those craving more of what they don't have. Extra protection as you ascend is essential against hostile forces starving for that power. Below is a list of some of the many benevolent deities that you can call on if you search for extra protection, guidance, training, or personal support. These beings are not only patient and loving but will impress you with their capability to guide, defend, deflect, and protect.

- Archangel Michael
- Archangel Gabriel
- Archangel Raphael
- Archangel Uriel
- Egyptian God Ra (the sun god)
- Egyptian God Horus
- Egyptian God Osiris
- Egyptian God Anubis
- Egyptian God Thoth
- Egyptian Goddess Isis
- Egyptian Goddess Hathor
- Egyptian Goddess Bastet
- Egyptian Goddess Maat

- Hindu God Shiva
- Hindu God Ganesh (or called Ganesha)
- Hindu God Vishnu
- Hindu God Brahma
- Hindu Goddess Parvati
- Starseeds
- Ascended Masters
- Jesus Christ (Yehoshua)
- Animal Spirit Guides
- Your Ancestors
- Dragon Spirits
- Mermaid Spirits
- Fairy Spirits

Metaphysical Benefits:
Spirits aligned in love and positive energy will benefit your spiritual journey greatly. If you need some guidance in something minor or to the degree of a more serious situation, they will help you. These deities and those like them will guide you in emotions, thoughts, magick, protection, spiritual warfare training, safe dimensional travel, psychic enhancement, breaking curses, and hexes, etheric cord-cutting, spirit reunion with departed loved ones, astral projection, love and so much more.

How to Call and What to Expect:
As everyone has their own belief in how to summon a deity properly, this all comes down to you and your personal preference. Benevolent deities don't require anything more than an honest heart and humility when asking for their help. You can call on them in a simple prayer or a ritual with their sigil, symbol, picture, or favored scent (resin, herbs, candles, etc.).

When summoning a deity, it's customary to speak of their name and ask what it is you seek. They don't require offerings of any kind, which is often debated. The best offering one could ever offer is your love, respect, and honor to the spirit. As they are shedding light, love, and respect to you, so should your love be reciprocated. What truly matters is you feel it's respectful and loving.

When you call onto these high ascended beings, be aware of your psychic senses and how you feel during the call. The moment the entity manifests, they will show their presence in several ways. You may see the entity in your third eye and envision the spirit in your home and talking to you or sense a powerful energy shift in the space. Sometimes they will appear to you in your bedroom in dreams or take you to another realm to meet them positively. There is absolutely no limit to how an ascended being will present themselves. Their core focus is to approach you in how it will be most comfortable and easily detectable to you. The manifestation is usually based on the living person's capability to sense and detect the spirit's presence.

When to Call:
There is never a better time than when you feel you need their loving guidance, protection, and support. They are never annoyed by your loyalty and respect as long as their goodness is not taken for granted. Keep in mind these spirits are not mindless entities. They possess their consciousness to decide to manifest to your call or not. If you don't receive their assistance as requested after a few days, take a moment to listen to your intuition to find the root of the cause. Sometimes a Spirit will appear that is different from the one you called. If this happens, kindly ask the current spirit why this occurred. Be sure to sense the energy of every spirit you encounter, whether summoned intentionally or not. If you ever feel threatened, uneasy, nervous, and uncomfortable in any way -call onto another deity you know will come to your protection, for this spirit may be a deceiver.

HOW TO BREAK A CURSE OR HEX

Although I believe that the best revenge is living a successful life, you cannot do that if Black Magick has burned you. Thankfully, I've been successful in breaking curses and sending the sender their due. When a curse or a hex has been cast against you, you may feel different, as if something dark and dooming has overwhelmed your entire sense of being. This psychic energy can be excessively uncomfortable to the point it causes severe depression, anxiety, panic attacks, bad happenings, nightmares, paranormal activity, sudden addiction, and more. Despite popular opinion, this evil stream of negative energy from a curse or a hex can not only be reversed but can even be sent back to the caster as a Karmic consequence!

To successfully break a curse, it's best to do so with at least one trusted benevolent Spirit Guide (Deity) who is highly skilled in magick and breaking curses or hexes. Whether you're breaking a singular curse/ hex or a generational curse, the process through required psychic intention and absolute focus remains the same. Of course, there is broad debate about breaking a curse or a hex. Still, I've discovered after years of successful astral exorcisms that one's intention and focus for the desired outcome is all that truly matters.

Having at least one material item representing the evil caster will assist in your mental stimulation and intent. A picture, name of the caster or even just the image in your mind can be enough. If you don't know who is responsible for your potential curse, you can still break the curse in the following.

In complete silence and uninterrupted focus, light at least one candle, either white or black. White candles represent the light and love of the universe, whereas black candles represent darkness and evil that you wish to banish. It doesn't necessarily matter what color candle you choose, as long as the color feels right to you when breaking a curse or a hex. If you feel drawn, you may use a black candle to represent the evil sent and a white candle to represent the good you desire back into your life. Using a candle ignites the intent you want to manifest with the flame as your guide in meditation to your third eye.

When you have the candle(s) safely lit, take your time to meditate and speak of what you want to happen. Writing down your spell's intention is equally essential to assert your verbal and written request to the universe. Write down how the magick helped in breaking the spell. Always write down your spell in the present tense as if it already happened. Doing this will ignite a psychic call to your Higher Self and the universe for your well-being of what it is you truly desire. Trust in yourself as you command for the curse or hex to be broken. Believing in yourself and help from your Spirit Guides is crucial when conducting a spell such as this. A large amount of energy depends on you to make this spell not only successful but also sent back to the one who cast the curse or hex. Visualize what you want to happen for you when the curse is broken. It's imperative to imagine during meditation how you feel, are, see, and taste in every sense of yourself when the curse is broken. Then when you feel your magick is successful, end your meditation with the image of the person who cast the curse and send it back to them.

Sending the curse back to the caster is optional, but it's highly recommended to teach the person a lesson. Karma isn't always what we think it is; sometimes, Karma happens when we decide it to be in the name of love, justice, and harmony. When the curse has broken, you may begin to feel different, lighter in the sense of energy, mind, body, and spirit. When the spell is complete, it's good to write down when you did this spell in a journal and how. Then pay close attention to your daily life and experiences and see if it seems to be working. Depending on the severity of the curse, the positive and visible signs may or may not be evident at first. Take time to view your life from a new perspective with faith that the curse is broken and you are protected by divine love. If you need a sign that the curse or hex has been lifted (broken), kindly ask your Spirit Guides to give you a sign or several signs.

You can also use white or black candles to banish negative or unwanted energy in the space of your room or home. Simply by lighting the candle and commanding your space to be cleared of harmful energies either written on paper, saying this aloud or by thinking it intently within your mind will help to force this intention into manifestation.

Calling for help from one of the deities or the type of Spirit you're drawn to is never a bad idea. These and countless others will answer your call when you feel you need the extra guidance, protection, or support. However, it's important to note that not all entities in the exact likeness are benevolent. For example, not all Dragon Spirits are kind, and not all Fairy spirits are super friendly. However, the deities represented by name are highly benevolent, as I've been working with these entities for years. Therefore, listening to your intuition won't fail you as long as you take time to learn the energetic vibrations of the deities listed and many that aren't.

What has been provided is for your reference and guide in hopefully the right direction towards psychic protection and purification. Of course, there will be mistakes, and you will be bruised along the way. That is for sure. No one is immune to spiritual warfare. However, as long as you continue to fight for your freedom and remain confident in your power in your Higher Self, you will come out stronger, braver, and unstoppable!

PSYCHIC EMPOWERMENT

CHAPTER NINE

Raising your vibration is not only adamant in establishing proper defense but also the psychic's metaphysical responsibility. The further you grow into your powers and psychic skills, the greater your chances of attracting unsolicited attention. This is why this helpful information may help ascend your eternal frequency to shape towards one's higher sense of security. Every aspect of who you are is cosmic and bountiful with the love and guidance of the universe. Where you feel you lack, the universe will teach. Where you think you need, the universe will provide. As stated in the law of duality, there are negative and positive vibrations: light and dark energy. Dark energy is neither evil nor 'bad,' which is true. However, dark forces refuse to accept that duality as its counterpart, thus wreaking havoc on those who accept and walk in the light. True power is birthed from beyond the depths of energy itself. From the heart chakra is directed and casted emotions. The stronger your feelings are towards what is good and loving, the more powerful your energy and shielding becomes. Therefore, establishing and surrendering to your Higher Self and intuitive guidance is where absoluteness remains. Securing inner peace through divine unity will help your sacred Higher Self provide the armor you seek.

To maintain the positive vibrations and guard your aura productively daily, I've provided ways in the following. The key to excellent metaphysical protection is to do your best to remain positive in mind, body, and spirit, including thoughts, emotions, behaviors, and lifestyle. Just like a flower garden cannot grow without receiving water and sunlight, you, too, should treat yourself with the proper love and care.

WAYS TO RAISE YOUR VIBRATION

- Receiving emotional healing by expressing and releasing emotions healthily and lovingly.

- Surround yourself with those who are like-minded. Your vibe attracts your tribe, so remain aware of those you spend valuable time. Those who resonate with you should make you feel energized, optimistic, upbeat, hopeful, faithful, and happy.

- Only assert yourself in safe and positive situations and activities. Avoid dangerous, reckless, and mindless illegal, unkind, and unsafe actions.

- Avoid drama and those prone to dramatic behaviors and personality traits. Unfortunately, empaths easily tune into the drama, so it's vital to remain aware of your emotions, thoughts, and personality.

- Watch positive films, television shows, etc. Watching something scary isn't necessarily going to lower your vibration instantaneously; however, it's crucial to limit horror flicks involving gore, rape, murder, paranormal, etc. Demonic entities are attracted to violent entertainment, so it's critical to determine how often one exposes themself to dark-centered films/television shows, etc.

- Receive therapy by a licensed psychologist or therapist as instructed or guided. There's no shame in asking for help from an expert. The more one can shed emotional baggage from past pains and sorrows, the brighter your aura gleam in eternal restoration. However, if you're like me and don't feel comfortable speaking to a stranger, asking for therapy from Spirit Guides will be just as beneficial to your mental and emotional health.

- Meditate daily. Meditation strengthens the bond within your astral body and with your Higher Self. The more frequently you can meditate, the higher your vibration will ascend. Meditation is considered a moral high ground. Doing so helps ground your astral body within the physical body and earth while simultaneously bonding a divine relationship with your Higher Self and the universe. The more you meditate, you will slowly feel vibration surge through your entire being and eventually learn to control it. This energetic vibration is your Higher Self and your source of celestial power. Getting in touch with yourself is where the magick happens.

- Get proper sleep. Sleep is what your physical body needs to maintain your livelihood and your psychic defense mechanics. So, if you feel your body needs a nap, or sleep longer or earlier, listen to what your body is telling you. Your body is also guided by your celestial body that is divine and loving and attached for you to experience the respected aspects of what it means to be physically alive temporarily.

- Maintain proper hygiene. Let's face it; this shouldn't be on the list. If you don't take showers at least every two days, then it may be time you should. No one likes a smelly person, nor should you want to be that person. (I tend to be sarcastically silly) In seriousness, if you tend to neglect your hygiene and aren't cleaning your body or shaving as often as you feel you should or like, do so for self-love. Proper bathing is necessary for itself, for a clean body helps maintain a pure mind and emotions.

- Listen to positive and uplifting music. As the eyes are the window to the soul, music is like the hymn of one's emotions. Listening to music full of hate, revenge, anger, and violence can toxify one's emotional database and mental images. Too much negativity in the ears can disdain thoughts of yourself and those around you. Listening to music grounded in love, joy, gratitude, confidence (not ego), and courage (not hate or revenge) will raise your vibration immensely. Rap and Hip Hop, for example, can be toxic and easily susceptible to mental manipulation if one doesn't keep the ego in check.

- Maintain a healthy diet. Eating junk food daily or sporadically is not going to affect your vibration. A soda, candy, or even take-out doesn't ultimately navigate your vibration when done in healthy moderation. If you believe being a vegan or vegetarian raises your vibration, then, by all means, live by that diet and lifestyle. However, a vegan and a vegetarian diet don't make one higher vibrational. I'm a meat-eater, and I've ascended to the 7th dimension. By eating grains, healthy carbohydrates, vegetables, water, etc., while moderating sugar with proper exercise, you can get positive results. Always listen to your nutritionist and medical physician when picking an appropriate plan of diet that works, as everyone's body is different.

- Get plenty of physical exercise. Of course, my exercise plan may not resonate with your physical and health needs, so it's essential to do what's best for you. Exercise just a few times a week will significantly increase your physical mobility and capabilities and increase your stamina and psychic defenses. The stronger you feel physically, the more you can maintain a positive mind, increasing confidence.

Science has discovered that meditating on running, for example, stimulates the same muscles in the body that use the exact muscles to move those body parts. So, if you're unable to be more physically active due to mobility restrictions, a meditation on those actions will be just as helpful. As the mind can create precisely what the astral body needs, those with physical disabilities are not without immense and equal exercise through the mind.

- Limit drugs and alcohol. Relax; you can still enjoy your favorite beer, wine, or liquor; however, it's imperative to moderate the amount of consumption. Illegal drugs and too much alcohol significantly decrease one's aura defense and frequency. Lower vibrational spirits like evil earth-bound spirits, demons, devils, and other familiar entities are attracted to lower-level intoxicants. Maintaining a clean and healthy mind is crucial when seeking to secure a spiritual foundation and forcefield. The last thing one wants is to be tempted by the devil when under alcohol or drugs. Those under the influence of drugs or alcohol are more easily influenced by negative spirits as the substances significantly decrease one's vibration and psychic defense. So, whenever willing, it's recommended to drink alcohol (those legally of age) when you're in a state of celebration, joy, love, and happiness. It's too easy to be consumed by negative emotions when taking in a lower vibrational drink. The higher and more positive one's mental state and feelings, the less likely one will be easily subjected to negative spirits or toxic vibrations.

- Spend quality time with loved ones. Remember, you're here for a reason. Though we are incarnated here to remember to find and regain our higher self, we are also here to enjoy the human experience. As technology advances, we quickly forget the beauty and pleasure of the little things like going to a friend's house and spending time with our pets and family. Taking time out of the week to remind others how much you care about them is a healthy and substantial mental therapy from the stress of the world, doubts, and worries.

- Remember to laugh it off! Sometimes laughing at the silly things is the best medicine. Laughter is considered in medicine to be the best medicine for a reason. Negative thoughts manifest into chemical reactions that are known to affect the body by bringing more stress and decreasing immunity. As a result, laughter makes life a little easier, especially when coping with difficult situations and emotions. Laughter may also ease pain by causing the body to produce natural painkillers.

- Have a healthy sex life. As hard as this is to believe, spirits encourage a healthy sexual lifestyle. Sex is not just an earth activity. Beings like Angels, Goddesses, and Gods reserve the privilege and the right to enjoy a healthy sexual relationship with their intimate partners. Beneficial sexual experiences raise the Divine Feminine and Divine Masculine energies allowing both parties to raise their vibrations charged in love and sensual intimacy. This includes gay and transgender relationships. Love isn't labeled in the higher realms and is encouraged to explore your sensuality concerning yourself and your partner. Those who don't currently have a partner can still independently raise their vibration in sexual pleasure. Aside from the controversy, you can have a healthy sexual relationship with a deity that is respectful, healing, and plentiful. Demons are NOT the only beings with sexual relationships with humans and, of course, are not encouraged as it's lower vibrational. However, Angels have relationships with incarnated humans to ease those in pain, assist in healing, and promote self-love while building a healthy bond. Sexual intimacy grounded in love, respect, and divine unity is highly beneficial and high vibrational.

- Remember to clean the house. Cleaning your home will help to wash away negative residual energy like past emotions, arguments, stress, anxiety, and worry. The more your home is cleaned to wash away negativity, the better the environment will feel. Rearranging furniture, and donating what no longer is used, wanted, or needed can also significantly improve the vibrations of your home and space. This is often why people do the occasional 'spring cleaning' to maintain the clutter of the items and will declutter unnecessary energy and emotions. You'll not only like the new look, but you will feel better too.

- Get out in the sun. Spending a few hours outside in nature will significantly increase one's mental health and aurific vibration. Whether taking a quiet walk in your favorite park, mending your garden, or taking a swim will all help increase your psychic defense and emotional well-being.

- Limit your screen time. Have you ever sat in a waiting room and noticed that everyone has a screen at their nose? Modern technology has impacted the world in many positive ways. It helps people reconnect and discover knowledge at their fingertips; however, it's also forced the majority of the world to lose a sense of what is more important. Moderating the amount of screentime is necessary when intending to raise your vibration. Social media has its pros and cons; however, too much social media and the internet will decrease one's awareness of the present moment. It's easily toxic, especially when pulling out your phone during an intimate conversation, ceremony, dinner, spending time with your kids, or even a date. Simply deciding when to use your device and not will increase your sensibility, rationality, and respect for others' time, relationships, and vibration. The less you're on your tablet or device, the easier it is to also tap into your Higher Self without the influence of social media, possible negative opinions, haters, and self-judgment.

VIBRATIONAL MYTHS AND MISCONCEPTIONS

Overall, it comes down to your opinion on what raises or lowers your vibration. No one can tell you what works for you and what doesn't. Even I won't tell you how to live your life and what is ultimately best for you. It's up to your judgment and intuition that will guide you on your spiritual evolution and protection path. However, there are indeed people who will attempt to spread lies and dangerous misconceptions on what ensures ascension, defense, and overall effects. Below are some of the more common misconceptions for further enlightenment against misguided solutions.

"Your Health Will Magically Improve!"

Whoever teaches this is a fraud! It's crucial to identify those that will try to sell you a 'positive solution' to your problems. Can raising one's vibration cause less 'dis-ease'? yes -but that doesn't mean you won't ever get sick. When diving into enlightenment, remaining logical and rational with a healthy dose of common sense is dire. Just because you visualize your aura as impenetrable from hostile psychic attacks doesn't mean you should walk out in the street to prove you can't get hit by a car. That's not only reckless but fatally unwise. We may be spiritual beings having a human experience, but we're not physically immortal.

"A High Vibrational Person Will Only Attract Positive Experiences"

Again, another genius idea that I've been forced to dismiss. Whosoever came up with this tagline needs a severe wake-up call. Those who find my responses egotistical have a problem with absorbing truths. It doesn't matter how positive one is or how loving you are; you can still be subjected to bad things. No one is immune to negative interactions, experiences, and even people. As long as there is negative energy, there are hostile people. And as long as there are negative vibrational people, there will be negative happenings and interactions. As long as you're aware of this and accept this unavoidable reality, you'll be able to maintain a healthy distance from toxic situations. Remember, Angels are some of the highest vibrational beings in the universe, and they still get into serious spiritual warfare.

"Your Vibration Attracts Equal Vibrations"

This is not entirely true and is downright disrespectful to those who experience abuse. That's like saying a dog that was hit by a car was the result of the dog's vibration. This is just another version of victim-blaming. This insensitive statement negatively affects the healing of not just one person but thousands -even millions of followers simply because of one misguided influencer. Everyone is indeed responsible for one's livelihood; however, those who prey on the vulnerable and the weak are responsible for evil happenings, not the victim.

Indeed, the vibration you give off can attract those around you, and at times the happenings but that doesn't and shouldn't ever blame those who receive a hit from an aggressor. Negativity manifests in many forms. Negative words, body language, thoughts, emotions, psychic attacks, and physical interactions reflect the sender, not the receiver! As an influencer, Psychic Medium, and Witch Goddess, it's disgusting to witness a spiritual 'guru' blame the victims subjected to harsh experiences. And it's my responsibility to remind you, dear universal brother, and sister, that you're not meant to control those around you through your vibration but to remain aware and protected. The more familiar you are with yourself through your intuitive guidance and psychic senses, the better you'll be at detecting when danger is near and shielding from cosmic threats.

Suppose positive thoughts, vibrations, and intentions are what secure and ensure one's psychic defense from hostile forces. So why do we see all these psychic channels, spiritual teachers, and influencers continually introduce new and 'practical' psychic protection products every few weeks? If raising one's vibration is needed to secure one's psychic protection and overall security, why do they keep insisting that you buy their psychic protective merchandise? Is it because they're trying to make an extra buck or because they know spiritual warfare is a metaphysical and undeniable reality!

THE LAW OF COMMAND

Although the previous universal laws mentioned, Law of Attraction and the Law of Free Will sizably affect one's life; your primary power source is in the assertive mental and energetic motion through the Law of Command. The Law of Command is a desired initiation from a willful decision to protect, honor, and maintain one's existence. Within everyone is a consciousness capable of making choices best suited for one's livelihood. Inside the magnificent galaxy of one's inner being is a spark of dignity and salvation awaiting permission to be set free to protect and defend your vital force. In short, you have a right, aside from the insatiable magnitude, to banish anything that deems unworthy of your energy source. You're the most excellent piece of creation gifted with a power that manifests what you desire and what you undoubtedly deserve! Where the Law of Command lies relies on you. The Law of Free Will gives everyone a choice in how to choose to live and be, and the Law of Attraction grants all the freedom to experience through that free will in desire. But it is in the Law of Command where you're gifted the psychic power to welcome goodness and banish wickedness.

POWER IN LOVE

Now and then, you will face an adversary, but it is ultimately up to you how you will handle it. At the end of the day, you're going to have to make a choice. You can abide by the threats and allow those who mean you harm to take control, or you can stand your ground and assert yourself with confidence and courage. It's not always easy, and I know this all too well. I've experienced some of the worst types of physical, psychic, and astral attacks that typically causes a person to commit suicide or completely lose their mind. There's no need for exaggeration. Each lesson can be obtained from something negative, and it is within one's view that counts. You can either observe through the eyes of a victim or as a survivor. And although you'll forever have the assistance and divine protection from the otherworldly benevolence, it's critical to understand and accept your ultimate potential. You are not only fully capable of banishing anything and everything metaphysically independently. Still, you can learn to harness and sustain that level of God-like benevolence the more you grow into your Higher Self. Once you've surrendered the ego and cleansed from the shadow of doubt, your celestial power is unleashed. True power doesn't come without first integrating into one's Higher Self through the will of acceptance of everything you are to release and banish evil forever.

Everything that has been provided is meant to permit you toward a higher sense of awareness of the unknown through energy detection and psychic protection. Although it would be nice to live a life through rose-colored glasses, it's better to take them off and accept the truth, as I'm sure that's why you purchased this book. Acquiring knowledge comes with a pearl of centered wisdom, knowing when to assert that knowledge through the lens of acceptance. Grounding yourself in love and positive thoughts and faith guides one towards an accelerated trust in courage and defense. The more you learn about yourself, the more you'll recognize your strengths and weaknesses. No one is immune to the hostility of the unholy, which is why it's necessary and required to accept these realities and defend against them at all costs.

Utilizing the tools and tips presented will better assist in daily defense against dark forces while empowering your aurific field.

When applying these protective barriers and methods, I not only hope you're better able to identify when potential metaphysical danger is near but know how to better protect against it. Trusting in yourself is where true power lies, and no one, not even the devil, can take that power away from you.

More work by Melinda available at Amazon.com

WORLD-RENOWNED
PSYCHIC MEDIUM, DEMONOLOGIST AND ASTRAL EXORCIST

MELINDA KAY LYONS

Demons And Familiars

A CONTEMPORARY GUIDE OF DEMONOLOGY

YOUR OPINION MATTERS

As an independent author and producer, it's always my mission to bring further enlightenment and enrich your spirit to a higher sense of self. If you enjoyed this book and found something good from it, your review on Amazon will help others in search of the same. All reviews are greatly helpful, appreciated and are received in gratitude.

Love,
Melinda the Mystic Witch